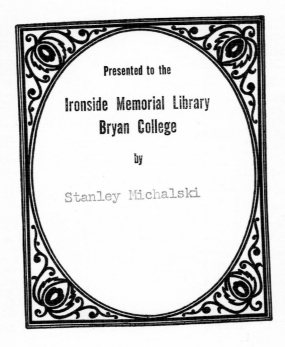

30-6

CHARLES E. PALMER

The Church

and the

Exceptional Person

PUBLISHED FOR

The Cooperative Publication Association

BY

A B I N G D O N   P R E S S

NEW YORK   NASHVILLE

THE CHURCH AND THE EXCEPTIONAL PERSON

Copyright © 1961 by Abingdon Press

THE COOPERATIVE SERIES

Leadership Training Texts

Many thousands of lay workers in Protestant churches attend
interdenominational leadership education schools each year. It is
essential that the courses offered and the text materials used be
acceptable to the many varieties of Protestant groups found in
our American communities.

The Cooperative Series of leadership education textbooks are
produced to meet that need. They are planned by the Division
of Christian Education of the National Council of the Churches
of Christ in the U.S.A., representing thirty-nine Protestant denominations. The Cooperative Publication Association, an interdenominational group of denominational editors and publishers,
selects the writers and provides editorial supervision to insure
sound educational values, practical usefulness, and interdenominational approval and acceptance.

SET UP, PRINTED, AND BOUND BY THE
PARTHENON PRESS, AT NASHVILLE,
TENNESSEE, UNITED STATES OF AMERICA

Preface

THIS BOOK HAS BEEN WRITTEN IN THE HOPE THAT IT WILL increase the reader's understanding of the characteristics, problems, and needs of exceptional persons. An effort has been made to avoid professional jargon and to use terminology which, though no less accurate, is more meaningful to the layman.

Recognizing that "a little learning is a dangerous thing," it is hoped that this book will be only the beginning of your search for understanding. Without understanding, the most elaborate plans are useless; with greater understanding, you can help the church make increasingly effective efforts to meet the needs of exceptional persons. Furthermore, as an individual you can do much toward eliminating frustration and heartache from the lives of those who are handicapped.

The author is indebted to writers, lecturers, and co-workers in the field of special education, as well as to teachers and parents of exceptional children for many of the ideas expressed and the suggestions offered.

Special thanks should be expressed to my wife for criticizing and editing the manuscript as the writing progressed, and to John W. Kidd of Northwestern State College for his suggestions and encouragement.

C. E. P.

Contents

Introduction

IT IS PARTICULARLY GRATIFYING TO ME THAT THE NATIONAL Council of the Churches of Christ should have chosen such an eminently qualified person as Charles E. Palmer to author this notable work. For not only is Dr. Palmer an expert in the field of speech pathology, holding the Ph.D. degree from the University of Wisconsin and Advanced Certification from the American Speech and Hearing Association, but he has been a student of theology, he has been a supervisor of special education, and, as much as any professional worker I know, he exhibits the true Christian spirit in his devotion to serving his fellow men.

After a quarter century of professional work with exceptional persons, Dr. Palmer has both theoretical understanding and practical "know-how." He writes in a chatty, easy-to-read style, but succeeds in condensing much pertinent information into the limited space of this volume.

This book, which I have had the pleasure of studying quite thoroughly, should be of real assistance to all teachers who are attempting to meet the needs of exceptional persons.

JOHN W. KIDD, *Ed.D., Director*
Special Education Center
Northwestern State College
Natchitoches, Louisiana

CHAPTER I

Why Are We Concerned?

> America has made a promise to the children of this
> country, a promise that all of them—the bright, the
> handicapped, and the "average"—will enjoy equal op-
> portunity to learn, that all will have full opportunity
> to reach their full measure of growth. Whatever our
> shortcomings in fulfilling this promise, the commit-
> ment stands as our ideal.[1]

"BROOKFIELD OPENS SPECIAL ROOM." "RETARDED TO HAVE
Special Class." "Special Teacher Hired at Hartland." These
news captions appeared in one county in one week. They
are evidence of the increasing effort being made throughout
the country to fulfill our commitment—to provide for the
needs of the exceptional person, the person who, to a significant degree, is different. Through special classes, through
special help in regular classes, and through night classes,
our public schools are making a determined effort to meet
the needs of all educable persons.

Recognition of the worth and rights of the person who
is exceptional is a fairly recent development. As we consider the relationship of the church to those individuals
who have exceptional needs, it may be well for us to begin
by tracing the changes in attitudes that have led to the
rapidly expanding program of special services today.

Primitive peoples had to struggle for survival. Weakness
could not be tolerated; the handicapped were rejected.

---

[1] John W. Kidd, "Special Education—Fulfillment of a Promise," *The
Elementary School Journal*, LVIII, 8 (May, 1958), pp. 454-56. Copyright 1958
by the University of Chicago Press. Quoted by permission.

They were cast from a precipice, drowned, buried alive, or abandoned in the forest. Even as recently as New Testament times, the blind and the crippled were left outside the city walls to wail with the lepers—rejected.

Gradually, the handicapped person came to be regarded as a source of humor. Wealthy noblemen vied with one another in providing entertainment for their guests; no feast was complete without the deformed jesters and buffoons. Sometimes those with speech defects were displayed in cages and, for a coin, would be prodded into talking for the amusement of the spectators.

In time, pity or pseudo pity became the accepted cultural reaction to those with handicaps. In some areas alms were so freely given that some children were deliberately deformed and trained to be beggars.

Helpfulness a Recent Development

The attitude of helpfulness has developed only recently. Although there is a record of sporadic efforts to teach deaf persons as early as A.D. 700, the schools opened in Edinburgh and Paris toward the close of the seventeenth century were probably the first institutions of their kind.

In America, it was not until 1815 that there was an organized effort to teach the deaf. At that time in Hartford, Connecticut, a group of citizens raised a small sum of money and used it to send a young minister named Thomas H. Gallaudet to Paris for a year to learn methods of teaching deaf children. Upon his return, the American Asylum for the Deaf was opened.

Early efforts to educate children with intellectual, physical, or emotional differences took the form of residential schools or asylums. Even these fell far short of today's goal. Today we believe that each exceptional person should receive the specialized education that will help him become a self-respecting individual who has the satisfaction of contributing to the welfare of the group. It was not until 1893 that the Boston Industrial School for the Crippled was established. This was probably our first training school that recognized a person's need to be useful, even though handicapped.

Shortly after 1900 a change in emphasis became evident. No longer was it considered necessary to send all children who were handicapped to "training schools" or asylums where they frequently were not only out of sight but out of mind. Instead, public schools began to assume responsibility for educating all children. Special education programs began to develop in the larger city school systems. This plan enabled a child to live with his family and at the same time receive the special help that was needed. By 1911 more than 200 cities in the nation had made a beginning toward the development of local programs.[2]

World Wars I and II were of major importance in changing social attitudes toward disabilities and furthering special education programs. Let us consider two aspects of this phenomenon.

Many men were rejected at military induction centers because of minor, nonvisible physical disabilities. Because they had been accepted in their home communities before they were rejected by the armed services, they were able to return to these communities as normal persons. Their friends knew that they "were different," yet continued to accept them as "normal." This slight modification of attitude perhaps made the second step easier.

During the war many men lost arms and legs, became paralyzed, lost their vision, or suffered impaired hearing. Before the war, these men had been thought of as capable laborers, competent teachers and physicians—leaders in the community. They had never been identified as belonging to the minority group of the exceptional. Although there were exceptions, when these men returned to their

---

[2] William M. Cruickshank and G. Orville Johnson, eds., *Education of Exceptional Children and Youth* (Englewood Cliffs, N. J.: Prentice-Hall, 1958), p. 14.

communities, most of their friends continued to regard them as "normal," but with-a-disability. In other words, the community began to look upon physical disabilities much more realistically—with more acceptance and less rejection. Gradually, and unconsciously, this healthy attitude was extended to include children as well as veterans, and mental as well as physical differences.

Parents Begin to Organize

These changes in social attitudes were favorable for the formation of parent groups. Parents, of course, are part of a community and tend to reflect its attitudes. For many years, because of the community's attitude toward both the exceptional child and his parents, parents tended to shelter and overprotect, or to reject the exceptional child. In some cases an exceptional child was not acknowledged as a member of the family. The change in social attitudes in the direction of understanding and acceptance, however, enabled parents to discuss their problems more freely. As early as 1940, parent groups were being organized.

Probably the first to organize on a large scale were the parents of cerebral palsied children. Local, state, and even a national organization were soon created. Parents wanted treatment centers for their children. They energetically raised funds. They enlisted the help of doctors, speech pathologists, physical therapists, and other professional workers. They demanded legislation that would provide for treatment, research, and the training of professional workers in many fields.

Also quick to organize were the parents of children with retarded or deficient mental development. They have influenced not only local school boards, but state legislatures and Congress. Largely as a result of parent influence, the United States Department of Health, Education and Welfare has, since 1956, been conducting a program of research in mental retardation.

11

The parents of children with almost every kind of exceptionality have organized and are encouraging the medical and psychological research that will make possible more effective programs of special education. There are still many questions to which we do not now have the answers, but the search continues, and as discoveries are made by research teams, they will be translated into plans of action.

Interest in persons who are exceptional is reflected in the large number of organizations listed in the appendix of this book. Of special interest is the Council for Exceptional Children, a strong department of the National Education Association. It is composed of teachers, administrators, psychologists, doctors, and others who are interested in the education of children who are exceptional. Its journal, *Exceptional Children,* furnishes information concerning all categories of exceptionality.

There are a number of reasons for the rapid growth of educational provisions for persons who are exceptional. First, some taxpayers point out that it costs less to provide the education and training that will make an exceptional person self-supporting, or even partially so, than it costs to provide even minimal maintenance throughout life. We know from experience that many persons who are crippled, who have visual or hearing handicaps, who are mentally retarded, or emotionally disturbed can—with proper therapy, education, and training—become self-respecting, contributing members of society. From the selfish motive of saving dollars, some people favor special education.

A second reason for the growth of special programs is found in our concept of equality of opportunity. We each have the guaranteed right to "life, liberty, and the pursuit of happiness." This is understood to mean that each individual has a right to the kind of experience that will help him develop his personality and talents to the fullest.

A third reason is found in our culture's concern for the "good life." This does not mean simply "a chicken in every pot." Rather, as a society, we believe that each individual should participate to the limit of his ability in the community life—social, religious, recreational, and scientific. Not only does this lead to a happier, more stimulating life for the individual, it also leads to an enriched society. But to participate satisfactorily, exceptional persons may need exceptional training.

Demands of the Christian Faith

Undergirding some of the above reasons is a fourth and basic reason—our Christian faith. As Christians, we have the teachings of Jesus, who urged compassion for all the disabled and insisted that all men are their brothers' keepers. Confronted with this religious heritage, civilized man found that pity tinged with revulsion was not enough; nor was the giving of alms. The Christian conscience is persistently irritated by the problems of the person with a handicap, and it has ruled in favor of the personal worth and dignity of the individual regardless of abilities or disabilities. We have reached a point where it is often said that the best index to the civilization of a community is what it does for persons who are exceptional.

Although it is true that our cultural attitudes toward these persons have changed from rejection, to humor, to pseudo pity, and finally to one of Christian understanding and helpfulness, the old patterns of reaction have not entirely disappeared. Every exceptional person has encountered rejection, mockery, and pseudo pity. We will give more attention to the way these primitive reactions affect the person in other chapters. Right now, let us examine our own attitudes in the light of social trends and in the light of the attitudes and teachings of Jesus.

It is rather puzzling to observe that, in spite of the important role that religion has played in the development of attitudes that made special education programs possible, the public schools—not the church schools—have led the way. There are probably several reasons for this. For one

13

The church must provide the religious motivation for concern about the exceptional person.

thing, the incidence of many types of exceptionality is relatively small. That means that many of our smaller congregations will have few, if any, persons with any one type of exceptionality. Another factor is the compulsory school attendance laws which called the attention of the public schools to the presence of children with exceptional needs. Since our church schools have made no special provision for persons with exceptional needs, these persons simply did not attend, and so constituted no gnawing problem. Still another factor is related to the growth of college programs for preparing teachers to work with exceptional persons. Schoolteachers and administrators were thus made more aware of the needs of persons who are handicapped.

The Church Must Motivate

There are some good reasons why public schools have led the way in serving the exceptional needs of children and youth, but the schools make no effort to serve in some

14

exceedingly important areas—indeed, they cannot. We may look to the schools to develop human abilities and skills, but the church must provide the religious motivations and insights that determine, in large measure, how these abilities are used. Inspiration, fellowship, a sense of direction, awareness of the reality of God, redemption, salvation, and deliverance *from* the feeling of futility *to* the inner joy and peace that Jesus promises—all that the church has to offer is needed by the minority composed of exceptional persons as well as by the majority that make up our congregations. We cannot escape the question, "When did we see you in heavy braces, or stuttering, or deaf, or blind, or confused, and rejected you?"

Let me tell you a true story. I was to preach at a little church hidden deep in the mountains. In spite of the creeks I had to ford, I reached the church in time for Sunday school. The adult class was discussing the thirteenth chapter of the Gospel of John, and the discussion became quite heated when they reached the fourteenth verse: "If I then, your Lord and Teacher, have washed your feet, you also ought to wash one another's feet." Inevitably, I was asked for my interpretation. I explained that in those days people wore sandals and walked in dusty roads. Just as today we give our guests an opportunity to "freshen up" after a journey, in those days an opportunity was given the guest to wash his feet. To honor a guest, the host washed his guest's feet for him. I went on to say that it seemed to me Jesus was saying that we should be glad to do anything that would contribute to the comfort and well-being of others, no matter how menial the task.

One bonneted old lady rose to her feet and declared vehemently, "I don't agree with you. If Jesus said we ought to wash one another's feet, we ought to do it. I really believe in it." She sat down, and then murmured, "But I ain't never done it."

Is it possible that some of us are like this woman? We believe we are obligated to serve, however menially,

15

wherever there is a need. We believe that all men are our brothers. We believe that every individual has the right to the Christian education that will help him develop his personality—his spirit—to the fullest. We believe that we are serving God when we serve our fellow men. We are willing to appropriate money to employ someone to teach a class for exceptional children in the public schools, but we are unwilling to become personally involved. We are unwilling to pay the price in terms of time—time to learn how to deal with various problems and time to replace our feelings of aversion with feelings of acceptance.

Because of people like you who are taking time to study the problems, the picture is changing. Churches throughout the country are taking steps that will lead to their assuming a greater place of leadership in serving the needs of exceptional persons.

In October, 1957, the Commission on General Christian Education of the National Council of Churches arranged for a consultation on the churches' responsibility for the Christian education of exceptional persons. It was held on the American Baptist Assembly grounds at Green Lake, Wisconsin, with fifty-seven persons attending. Official denominational representatives, members of the staff of the National Council of Churches, representatives of state and national agencies, and a number of interested teachers and parents all joined forces to study the problem, to clarify their thinking as to what the Protestant churches should be doing toward the Christian education of exceptional persons, and to make specific recommendations.

Among other things, we learned from this consultation that in various congregations throughout the country, without ballyhoo or fanfare, provisions are being made for persons with exceptional needs. Since this consultation, some of the special arrangements have been reviewed in local newspapers. An increasing number of articles dealing with this subject are appearing in denominational journals and in the *International Journal of Religious Education*.

Groups are forming to study the problems involved and to determine what should be done.

Perhaps it is too early to proclaim that the church is on the march. But the church is certainly mobilizing its forces. Some congregations are already conducting special programs. Others are making plans to start. Throughout the country, church people are saying, "Let the little ones come unto us—regardless of their limitations—for of such is the kingdom of heaven."

Those who have taken the time to get to know and understand persons with exceptional needs have found that the experience has contributed to their own emotional and spiritual maturity. Making the effort to include exceptional persons in the program of the church has other valuable by-products. For one thing, those who become acquainted with persons who have been handicapped by epilepsy, cerebral palsy, blindness, or some other cause, learn what to do when help is needed. Some may become so interested that they will decide to enter one of the fields of service to those who are handicapped. (There are tremendous opportunities for Christian young people in these professional fields!) A nucleus of informed church members can also help to change the attitudes and increase the understanding of the general public. Finally, as members of the community learn to see through the handicap and its limitations to the person and his abilities, increased opportunities for employment will be made available to exceptional persons. A small beginning in your church can have far-reaching effects.

This book is intended to help you understand persons with exceptional problems and to suggest some possibilities you may want to try as you plan to extend your church's ministry to include each of God's children, whatever his abilities or limitations.

CHAPTER II

General Considerations

Before we try to define and describe the various types of handicaps or exceptionalities, let us consider some definitions and general principles that we will need to keep in mind.

The Meaning of "Exceptional"

In the preceding chapter the words "handicapped" and "exceptional" were used almost as though they were interchangeable. "Exceptional" is the broader term. A man may be exceptionally tall or exceptionally short. In either case we may say that his height is exceptional—it differs from the average to a significant degree. Whether his exceptional height is a handicap depends upon the task or activity to be attempted. If he is exceptionally short, his height may be a handicap in trying to win a place on a basketball team. If he is exceptionally tall, his height may be a handicap in trying to get into a foreign-made car. In many areas, his height may be of no significance. The gifted child, the child with superior intellectual abilities, would be included in the classification of the *exceptional;* he may or may not be *handicapped* in some other area.

Perhaps this is a good place to remind ourselves that the "average" child simply does not exist. He has been referred to as "a figment of the imagination" and "a statistical nonentity." If Tom has six apples; Mary, eight; Sue, twelve; and Joe, fourteen, the average number of apples is ten. Yet no child in the list has ten!

Many human characteristics, such as height, weight, and

intelligence, vary along a continuum, with the largest number of individuals falling near the middle of the distribution. Let us consider height. If we group all men according to height, we find the largest number in the middle group. As we move from the center in either direction, we find fewer men in each group. At the end of the line (or continuum) on one side we have the one tallest man, and at the other end the one shortest man. By adding the heights of all the men measured, then dividing by the number of men, we obtain the mean—the average height. Let us assume that we find the average height of the American man to be 5 feet 9 inches. We would not say that a man 5 feet 8 inches or 5 feet 10 inches tall is "abnormal," handicapped, or exceptional. In fact, moving just a little way (one standard deviation, to use statistical parlance) in both directions from the average will include about 68 per cent of all of the adult male population. This group is usually referred to as "falling within the normal range."

The exceptional person may be thought of as a person who is outside the normal range; he does not belong in the large group that clusters about the average. The exceptionality may be an advantage or a disadvantage, or, in some circumstances, it may make no difference. A person may "fall within the normal range" of many characteristics and abilities, but be "exceptional" in one limited area.

The handicapped person not only falls outside the normal range; he has a limitation of some kind that prevents him from doing some of the things that the "average" person of his age and sex is able to do.

He is an individual. Whether he be mentally retarded, deaf, blind, emotionally disturbed, defective in speech, or multi-handicapped, the exceptional individual is, first of all, a person. He has the fundamental needs that are common to all of us. He gets hungry, thirsty, and sleepy. But more important, he needs love, understanding, companionship, and self-expression. He needs both security and a sense of adventure. He needs the satisfaction that comes only through making a contribution to his group. He needs a realistic appraisal of himself as an individual of personal worth, along with the feeling that he is accepted and "belongs."

These needs are common to all of us. To repeat, the person who is exceptional or handicapped is, first of all, a person. We must recognize the wide areas in which all children—or adults—are alike. We need to understand the "normal" growth and developmental problems before we can understand the growth and development of the person who is exceptional.

An Individual with a Difference

We do a disservice to the exceptional person if we fail to emphasize another point. The person who is exceptional is one with a difference. It is this *difference* that makes him *exceptional;* it is this difference that makes it difficult to supply all of his needs. The ways in which his needs can be fulfilled will vary with the limitations of the handicap, the nature of the exceptionality, and, of course, with the personality and varied abilities of the individual.

In the past, when the attitude of society was that of rejection or aversion, through lack of understanding of the many commonalities, it was necessary to stress the important areas in which the exceptional person is "just like everybody else." We need to keep the commonalities in mind and to remember that every exceptional person must be seen as an individual of worth and dignity. We cannot, however, understand the very problems we are attempting to solve unless we remember that the exceptional person is one with a difference or differences. These differences create the problems.

Special education exists in our public schools because some of the persons about whom we are concerned in

Special education exists because some persons have needs that cannot be met in the regular program.

this study have differences in needs that cannot be met in the regular school program. Special methods, special arrangements—sometimes special furniture and equipment—are needed.

Imagine the average or "normal" child in the center of a circle. As we move in any direction we encounter differences—differences in physical ability, mental ability, social adjustment, visual acuity, hearing acuity, facility in speech, or in some other area. The farther we move from the center of the circle (the so-called "normal"), the greater the differences that we encounter. If we move far enough from the center, we find a child who cannot see what the teacher has written on the chalkboard; move a little farther in that direction and we find a child who cannot read the book in large print on his desk. Move in other directions, and we find a child who cannot hear what the teacher says, and a child who cannot use speech to express himself, or a child who cannot stand up when the teacher calls his name.

Of course there is no one child who is the average or the

21

"norm" in every respect. There are many factors or variants, and we are all different. For a "difference" to be a handicap, the deviation from the norm must be great enough to make a difference—it must interfere with behavior that is considered "normal."

On each of the variables there are differences of degree or extent. A hearing loss may make no more real difference than a slight turn of the volume control on your radio, or it may blot out all sound—which *does* make a difference. Impaired speech may be no more significant than a slight lisp, or it may make speech unintelligible. A diagnosis of epilepsy may make no more real difference in a person's behavior than occasionally dropping a book and missing a sentence in the conversation, or it may require constant supervision and safeguards.

Beware of Labels

To understand what special needs a person has, it is necessary to know a great deal more than the medical diagnosis of "post poliomyelitis," or "epilepsy," or "cerebral palsy, athetoid." Any of these or other labels have been attached to many persons; but as we look at the people grouped under one of these labels, we find quite a variety. Not only does a good diagnosis attach a label to a disorder; it states (in so far as it is possible to determine) the etiological factors or causes. Even more important for us, interested as we are in working with the individual, a good diagnosis states the extent of the limitations, and prognosis predicts what may be expected. Although the label may be the same, the precise limitations and residual abilities that exist will be different for each individual.

You have known brothers or sisters, or even twins, and have marveled that they could have the same parents and, superficially at any rate, the same environment, and yet be so different. It should not surprise us, then, that even if two children of exactly the same age have precisely the same label attached, and (if you can imagine it) the same limitations and abilities, they will not be the same. They will not have the same disposition, they will not respond to all stimuli in the same way, they will not react to frustration, disappointment, or pleasant surprises in the same manner.

The main point of this part of our discussion is that we must not be blinded or prejudiced by labels. Each person *is* an individual. To determine the best way to help him, we, as teachers, must know all that we can find out about him. This is not to satisfy our curiosity, but because we know that a good teacher can help her pupils best when she knows all that it is possible to know about them. We must recognize that the person who is handicapped often has much in common with the so-called "normal" person; but he does have a handicap, and this makes some difference. How important this difference is will be determined partially by the extent of the handicap and by the personality, attitudes, and abilities of the individual.

Utilize Abilities

Remember the song that urges us to "accentuate the positive"? That is good advice for working with persons who are handicapped. To be realistic and to avoid causing unnecessary frustration, we must be aware of the limitations, but we must emphasize the abilities. This will require a careful evaluation of the individual. Having discovered his abilities, we will try to develop them, build on them, help him to use them.

Let us see how this works. The members of a class plan to raise money for some worthy project. They are going to sell tickets to a play. Joe, in his wheel chair, designs the posters; Susan, in her heavy braces, helps to paint them. Tom, who is mentally retarded, delivers the posters to merchants who have been persuaded (by a telephone call from Kate, who is visually handicapped) to display them. Mary, who spends hours each day in bed, is in charge of newspaper publicity.

23

Bill's crutches do not interfere with his duties as chairman of ticket sales. These children are not left out, nor are they given tasks which were obviously created for them. Each has the satisfaction of making a contribution to a worth-while group project. *Limitations must be recognized, but abilities must be utilized.*

A Common Denominator

We have been stressing the individuality of each person who is exceptional. In the next chapter we shall try to discover some common denominators for each group. There is one characteristic however, which in greater or lesser degree is likely to be found in all handicapped persons—frustration. Impaired speech and hearing loss interfere with communication, and communication is the basic tool for adjustment. A blind boy will never have the fun of driving a rebuilt 1929 car. A heart condition or a crippled limb may not permit some of the normal activities that are so important in companionship and human relations. It is no wonder that many persons who are handicapped live in a constant state of frustration—frustration that results from the attitudes of others toward the handicap as often as it does from the handicap itself.

Maintain Objectivity

After the specialists have done all that modern medicine and surgery can do to reduce the effects of the disorder or disability, the exceptional person must learn to live with his limitations. This statement does not reflect a lack of sympathy. It is an objective statement. It is realistic. There is no other way. We cannot help unless we realistically and objectively face the facts.

Of course we will try to be aware of the difficulties that the person has faced and be appreciative of any efforts he has made; but we will not let our sympathetic appreciation blind us to the realities of the situation. Disappointments and heartaches can best be minimized or avoided by the early recognition of the person's limitations and existing or potential *abilities*. A satisfactory adjustment by the person, his family, and his teachers can be achieved only when the facts are determined and acknowledged.

Provide Counseling

To achieve this desirable adjustment, most exceptional persons and their families will need a great deal of counseling. We will give more attention to the church school teacher and her role in another chapter. Just now, let us emphasize three points.

1. Counseling is needed at all ages. Frequently we make the mistake of thinking that only adolescents need counseling. But the five-year-old needs this help as much as does the fifteen-year-old, or the twenty-five-year-old, or forty-five-year-old who has a problem. The problem will differ, of course, but the need for counseling is present. Each of us has experienced difficulty in adjusting to some situations. The person who is handicapped may be expected to have more difficulty; hence, there is a greater need for counseling. The five-year-old who cannot run after a ball or climb the stairs as rapidly as his companions needs counseling. So does the forty-five-year-old who cannot talk because his larynx has been surgically removed. So does the sixty-year-old who has lost his hearing, or his sight, or his health. That is, each needs someone to help him understand the situation, evaluate it, and make an adjustment that will enable him to live as happily as possible with that limitation.

2. One of the goals of counseling is the development of a realistic, functional, self-concept. The person who is handicapped must be helped to set realistic goals—both for the present and for the future. He needs to develop self-appreciation, as well as appreciation of and respect for others.

I once heard a teacher of a class of mentally retarded children say, "You are just as good as anyone else. You can do anything they can do. It may take you a little longer, and you may need a little help—that's why I'm here. But if someone else can do it, you can." Now that just wasn't true. The older children in the class knew that it wasn't. The teacher may have been trying to encourage the children to apply themselves, but in the eyes of some of her pupils she was lying, and from then on they did not trust her. The younger children may have forgotten her statement by the time they learned "in life's hard school" that they just could not do what some children could, no matter how hard they tried.

We have stressed the point that our appraisal of the person with a handicap must be realistic. It is equally important that the person's appraisal of himself be realistic. Through understanding his limitations and abilities, we can anticipate problems that he is sure to face and, through counseling, help prepare him to meet them. By helping him develop a functional self-concept we can help him learn to face the rebuffs, the condescension, the rejection of those who do not understand.

3. Moral and spiritual values are important. Those who have discovered and accepted as their own the standard of values that Jesus used are happier people. The adoption of Jesus' standard of values is a long step toward the sense of fulfillment, the feeling of poise and contentment that our Master referred to as "the abundant life." Each of us needs a philosophy of life that recognizes spiritual realities, religious ideals, and Christian ethics. Included, of course, in a Christian philosophy is the recognition of the worth of the individual and the dignity of man whom God made but "a little lower than the angels." The person with a handicap has even greater need than most of us for such a philosophy of life. One of the objectives of counseling for the exceptional person is to help him develop a Christian philosophy of life.

"Is It My Fault?"

Parents of children with handicaps often ask such questions as, "What did I do wrong? Am I responsible for my child's condition? Why did God do this to me? Am I being punished for some sin of my own, of my husband (or wife), of our parents?" Experienced social workers tell me that during the hours of counseling these questions are asked sooner or later, but inevitably! How would you answer them?

Some of this questioning possibly arises from the often quoted passage, "For I the Lord your God am a jealous God, visiting the iniquity of the fathers upon the children to the third and the fourth generation of those who hate me" (Exodus 20:5). Many parents concentrate on this passage to the exclusion of the many references to God as forgiving, merciful, and compassionate.

One of the most vehement remarks I ever heard from a minister was: "I will neither worship nor serve because of fear! Any god I worship must be superior to the most kindly Christian gentleman I know. Since only thugs and hoodlums take pleasure in maiming innocent children, I know that the God I worship would have no part in it." He went on to say that he did not understand sin and suffering, but he had observed that scientists do not abandon their belief in a world of order just because they cannot always trace the laws of cause and effect.

We believe that our Creator is a loving, heavenly Father, but he is also a God of order. Life in a world without order is inconceivable. If the laws of the universe applied only in Alabama today and only in Arizona tomorrow, we would have chaos! Our situation would be improved but little if we lived in a world where some force or power kept interfering with the order of things and with the laws of cause and effect. The concepts of God as wise, rational, and dependable rest, at least in part, upon our observance of the order of the universe. The inevitability of these laws may

27

seem stern and uncompromising, but inevitability is essential to the very sciences that seek to relieve suffering. Ether (discovered as useful in surgery in 1842), insulin (1921-22), penicillin (1928 or 1929), Salk vaccine (1955), and all other medical and scientific advances are possible because of an orderly universe.

Although we do not fully understand God's laws, men with God-given intelligence have found ways of reducing the infant death rate per 1,000 live births from 99.9 in 1915 to 26.4 in 1959; the maternal death rate per 10,000 live births from 60.8 in 1915 to 3.6 in 1959; the tuberculosis death rate per 100,000 population from 113.1 in 1920 to 6.7 in 1959.[1]

Scientific research has not yet found the causes of many handicapping conditions. For example, it is known that if the palate is not formed by the end of the third month of embryonal development, a child will be born with a cleft palate; but precisely what interferes with normal development is not definitely established. Nevertheless, because we believe that this is a universe of order, we may hope that someday the exact cause of this and other handicapping conditions will be discovered and that we will learn what steps must be taken to prevent them.

No Reason to Blame God

There is always a cause, but there is never any reason to blame God. Usually there is no reason for parents to blame themselves. Even in those cases in which, perhaps through negligence, parents are clearly responsible, they must be urged not to waste time in self-recrimination or self-pity. Rather, let us help them to devote their energies to the discovery of God's laws of healing so that they may provide the proper care and treatment for their child.

One important step toward developing a functional

---

[1] These figures apply to the population of the United States of America and are taken from the *Statistical Abstract of the United States, 1960,* Bureau of the Census, Department of Commerce, pp. 61 and 65.

self-concept and satisfying adjustment has to do with the feeling of frustration that we discussed earlier. Frustration results from not being able to do the things that we want to do or that we think we are expected to do. On the other hand, confidence may be thought of as a feeling that we can perform satisfactorily whatever task is expected of us.

Develop Confidence

Anything that we do to help the person who is handicapped develop greater self-confidence will make the problem of adjustment easier for him. We may help in three ways:

1. Increasing ability results in increasing confidence. To a large extent this approach may be the responsibility of professional workers. For example, the task of increasing facility with speech must rest primarily upon the professional speech therapist (although there is much that the layman may do when guided by the professional). However, we may encourage our public schools to provide speech therapy adequate for the needs of our children. Much the same statements may be made of other areas. But through our evaluation of the individual, our sympathetic exploration, and imaginative attempts, we may discover ways to use existing abilities and encourage the individual to develop his talents. So often our attention is focused on the crutches, the hearing aid, or some other "badge of difference" that we fail to look for the existing abilities. It is through the discovery and development of his abilities that we may help an exceptional person develop improved self-concepts, achieve status in the group, and increase his self-confidence.

2. The second step in the development of self-confidence consists of setting goals realistically. There are two aspects of this step: the setting of goals by the teacher and parents, and the setting of goals by the person who is handicapped. The goals set for and by this person must be goals that he

29

can reach. Furthermore, they must be clearly defined so that he may know when they have been reached.

Not long ago I purchased an assortment of bulbs. The directions stated, "Plant at proper depth." Now to an experienced bulb-planter, perhaps that was clear enough. For me, it wasn't. The goal had not been clearly defined! Furthermore, long-term goals must be broken down into intermediate steps. It may be desirable to have these steps or goals graphically represented on a chart that the child may color or the adult can check as each one is achieved.

"Nothing succeeds like success" is not an original idea, but sometimes we forget it. Realistic goals, clearly defined, broken down into steps that may be achieved over a relatively short period of time help to give the person a feeling of progress, a feeling of self-confidence based on the experience of being able to do what is expected.

3. The third step toward self-confidence consists of attaching proper values to the goals that have been set. This is rather tricky business. Enough value must be attached to the goal so that it is worth working for, and so that achieving it becomes a stimulating, rewarding experience. At the same time, we must not attach, and we must not let the handicapped person attach, so much value to a goal that failure to attain it is a heartbreaking or traumatic experience. To be successful in helping a person attach just the right amount of value to a goal, we must be sensitive to individual needs. Often we must be indirect. Seldom is it possible to change a person's set of values simply by enunciating a different set.

Whenever I hear an adult refuse a child's request with a smug "You'll like this better," I remember an incident that occurred on a college campus. A beautiful redheaded senior was wearing a pink organdy dress. Her mother said with a wry smile, "When she was just a little girl she wanted a pink dress. I told her that she looked prettier in greens and browns, and she never mentioned it again. But I guess she never stopped wanting the pink dress."

A person may outwardly accept the values that others proclaim, but for purposes of adjustment this is not enough. Subtly, indirectly, we must help the person with a handicap set realistic goals and attach appropriate values to those goals.

Provide Acceptance

The individual with a handicap has to be accepted just as he is—handicap included. Without such acceptance he cannot develop self-confidence. Without self-confidence he cannot bring himself to put forth his best efforts, for he feels that even his best is not good enough. Fundamental to working with the exceptional person is the development, on our part, of an attitude of genuine acceptance based on an understanding of his problems and an appreciation of his difficulties.

Such acceptance eliminates both rejection and condescension. Most of us, at least until we are sufficiently mature to feel at ease in the presence of "differences," have to guard against the forced, artificial smile; the banal, inane remark; the "mother-hen" approach of oversolicitousness; and the "Old Faithful" approach of effusiveness (otherwise reserved for greeting infants).

A young man wrote to me from his wheel chair:

> Our needs are the same as those of anyone else, but the one most difficult to satisfy is acceptance. As the racial minority seeks dignity and recognition of the individual, so does the disabled minority. . . . Where a racial minority experiences hostility, we receive obsequious kindness. But killing the spirit with kindness, although more subtle, can be equally, if not more, effective than open hostility.

Some individuals admittedly are more pleasant to be with than others. Some have irritating mannerisms and undesirable characteristics. Sometimes the unattractive features

31

are directly related to the handicapping condition. For example, some persons who have cerebral palsy drool because they cannot control the muscles of the mouth and throat; some persons who are visually handicapped have a facial expression that seems to be a combination of a scowl and a smirk, but is actually the result of squinting in an effort to see you more clearly. Redheaded persons do not have a monopoly on temper any more than bald-headed persons have a monopoly on benevolence, or fat persons on humor. We will expect to find a wide variety of personalities, attitudes, and mannerisms in any group of people—including those who are in one way or another exceptional.

Acceptance of the individual is essential; it is not always easy. The Christian, however, believes in Jesus' promise that we will receive grace and strength sufficient for our needs if we ask in his name.

Since it is easier to accept when we understand, in the next chapter we will try to increase our understanding of various types of exceptionalities and in so doing, attempt to free ourselves of prejudice and feelings of rejection.

> "You will know the truth, and the truth will make
> you free." (John 8:32.)

CHAPTER III

Classification and Description

THERE ARE MANY CLASSIFICATIONS OF EXCEPTIONALITIES. IN our discussion we will use a classification which is often used in educational circles. We will discuss those who are intellectually exceptional (the gifted, the slow learner, the mentally retarded-educable, -trainable, and -custodial); those who have impaired hearing (the deaf, the deafened, and the hard of hearing); those who have impaired vision (the blind and the partially sighted); those who are crippled (or orthopedically handicapped); those who have defective speech; those who are emotionally disturbed; those who are multi-handicapped; those who are in institutions or are homebound. We will attempt to define each group, indicate the incidence of the exceptionality, and discuss some of the characteristics and special problems.

In some areas there is an abundance of literature and we will try to summarize in a few pages the data that will be most helpful. In other areas there has been little research and little is known. In most areas there is more reliable information about children than there is about adults, for it is relatively easy to conduct studies dealing with this segment of our population.

Regardless of the amount of research data available, let us be cautious! Remember that a person *is* an individual.

It is easy to attach a label to a group; it is extremely difficult to describe all of the abilities, limitations, and personality factors of any individual within the group. The characteristics ascribed to a clinical group may or may not be present in certain individuals within that group, and in others will be present only in varying degrees. Although there are widely accepted scales for assessing intelligence, and physical limitations may be accurately described in terms of neuromuscular impairment, there are other important factors that cannot be measured. Persistence, motivation, energy, and other factors must be considered. At present, in our efforts to predict successful adjustment or achievement, we have no way of calculating the relative values of different factors. There is no equation that enables us to say "one unit of persistence is equivalent to one-half unit of intelligence," or, "three units of motivation are equivalent to one unit of energy."

Lacking such formulas, we must secure all available information about a person and observe him as he functions in various situations. The following pages point out characteristics to which we may be alert, but we must really know the individual if we are to determine what educational plans are best for him.

I. THE INTELLECTUALLY EXCEPTIONAL

INTELLECTUAL ability follows the "normal distribution" pattern discussed in the preceding chapter. The majority of the population clusters around the average, and the number with a given score diminishes rapidly as we move away from the average range in either direction.

For purposes of classification, we must draw a line somewhere, but we need to remember that there is no magic in labels and that the distribution is continuous—that is, we do not find groups separated by wide gaps in ability. In some school systems one of the criteria for enrollment in a special class for the mentally retarded-educable is that the child have an I.Q. between 50 and 80. This is an arbitrary division. A person with an I.Q. of 80 is not noticeably different from a person with an I.Q. of 81, but he is significantly different from a person with an I.Q. of 50! In other words, he is more like some who have not been assigned to his group than he is like those at the other limit of his group. This is an important point to be kept in mind during the following discussion.

Definitions. The terminology used by various writers is confusing. Some authors use the term "slow learner" to designate those whom others refer to as "mentally retarded." Some writers divide the "mentally retarded" group into the "mentally handicapped" and the "mentally deficient." If you read an article or a book that deals with mental retardation, be sure to discover how the author defines his terms and the range of intelligence to which he refers.

I.Q. scores of 90 to 110 are usually thought of as representing the "normal range of intelligence." Those with higher I.Q. scores are sometimes referred to as "superior," "very superior," and "gifted." In our discussion we shall refer to anyone with an I.Q. above 125 as "gifted." On the other side of the average range there is a large group whom we shall call the "slow learners" (I.Q. 80-90). The next group we refer to as the "mentally retarded-educable" (I.Q. 55-80). The "mentally retarded-trainable" group is our designation for the next lower group (I.Q. 30-55). The last and smallest group we shall call the "mentally retarded-custodial" (I.Q. up to 30).[1]

No child should receive one of the above labels without thorough professional testing. The church-school teacher should not concern herself with I.Q. scores. The school psychologist or others may indicate that a child would benefit from inclusion in a special class, or that he should be thought of as having the mental abilities of a six-year-old (rather than the ten-year-old that he is). Or the teacher may be told that this child is mildly or severely retarded. Agencies do not give the I.Q. score to the parents. Unless through professional training the church-school teacher is capable of interpreting and using the I.Q. score, she should

---

[1] This classification for the mentally handicapped closely parallels the recommendations of the American Association on Mental Deficiency; however, the I.Q. limits differ slightly.

not ask for it. If she does receive it, it must be held in *absolute confidence*. I know of one public-school program for retarded children that collapsed simply because the teacher did not keep I.Q. scores "top secret." For our purposes the I.Q. is relatively unimportant. We want to know only whatever tests reveal that will help us understand the person's abilities and limitations.

A good psychological examination helps you know how to start making plans for the child who is mentally retarded.

The Gifted

The percentages given for the various types of exceptionality are, in some cases, estimates of national averages and will vary widely from community to community. Some school districts report from 3 to 29 per cent as gifted. In the light of various surveys, one may think of 7 per cent as a conservative estimate.

Characteristics. Persons in this classification have a wide variety of physical, social, and emotional characteristics, and they differ widely as to mental ability (some having I.Q.'s of 180 or higher) . As a group they tend to be a little

36

above average physically. The majority are friendly, outgoing, happy persons. (There are, of course, exceptions on every count.)

In their discussions of interests and activities, gifted children are often disconcertingly mature. They are quick to recognize insincerity and a lack of frankness, but often discern that it is not prudent to reveal their discovery to adults! They usually respond eagerly to an adult who reacts sympathetically and honestly to their discussions of problems, activities, and aspirations.

Problems. Because he learns more quickly and has more mature interests, the gifted child has a problem of adjustment to the less able child in his environment, and the adult leader (teacher or parent) has the problem of trying to keep him interested and motivated. The leader must find ways of keeping him busy with interesting, challenging activities, or he will find other outlets for his energies and abilities. Some of our so-called "delinquents" are gifted children who became bored with the activities of the groups to which they belonged. If the gifted child comes from a home or a neighborhood in which his exceptional ability is not understood and appreciated, the problems of adjustment are increased. Finding congenial companionship is a problem. A gifted child of ten may have the mental abilities of a "normal child of fifteen," but not many fifteen-year-olds welcome association with a ten-year-old; there are too many physical and social differences. Efforts must be made to bring together in congenial relationship children of similar mental abilities without too wide a spread in age.

These gifted children will be the leaders of our church and community if they are challenged in the church with opportunities equal to their abilities. Teachers and workers in the church school must be alert to recognize these persons and to evaluate their particular abilities. They will find this at least as difficult as their work with slow learners. But the goal is worth the effort.

The Slow Learner

Moving from the "normal range" of intelligence in the opposite direction from the gifted, we find the slow learners. This large group constitutes about 15 per cent of the public-school population.

Characteristics. Slow learners are usually the students who do the poorest work in the regular classroom, they work "below their grade level," and even when they work at their best they have difficulty in "keeping up." As a group, they are not much different from the "normal" or "average," but as we move away from the most able in this group toward the least able, we find that they have much in common with those who are mentally handicapped. For this reason, the characteristics and problems discussed in the next section will be found, to greater or lesser degree, in working with persons who fall toward the lower arbitrarily drawn limit of this group.

Mentally Retarded-Educable

Estimates vary from 3 per cent to 10 per cent for the number of our school-age population in this group. The estimate of 3 per cent is probably conservative.

Characteristics. These are the children who are sufficiently retarded to need special help in order to prepare for adult living. They learn more slowly, but with special education many of them can become self-supporting and self-respecting members of the community. Under favorable conditions they will be capable of managing their own affairs, but counseling will be needed from time to time—especially in periods of crisis.

These children may be a little smaller and have more than their share of physical defects, but they are not readily distinguished from their classmates except on the basis of intellectual growth. Their maximum mental age will be from nine to thirteen years.[2] They sometimes seem to have more than their share of behavior problems, but lack of emotional adjustment is usually the result of social and academic pressures with which they are unable to cope.

Problems. A mentally retarded-educable child has all of the needs of other children, including the need to compete successfully in at least some areas. These needs are not easily met in the typical classroom.

The expectations and pressures of society in general—and the classroom in particular—tend to destroy any feeling of confidence and worth, and condemn the child to a succession of failures and frustration. Some in this group quietly stop trying and withdraw to their own private worlds; others rebel. One girl, with surprising insight, said,

> I used to cry when I failed. Everybody knew that my best wasn't good enough. I was a nobody. Whenever they chose sides for anything I was the last one chosen. Then I began acting like I didn't care. I'd say silly things that made the teacher mad, but they made the kids laugh. I showed them I wasn't afraid of the teacher or the principal or anybody.

These children tend to have difficulty in grasping abstractions and generalizations. They usually do better when dealing with the practical and specific. Even in these areas they will be expected to make slower progress than their more able peers.

---

[2] The mental ages used here and in subsequent paragraphs are based on the I.Q. tables (pp. 257-58) of *Stanford-Binet Intelligence Scale—Manual for the Third Revision* by Lewis M. Terman and Maud A. Merrill (Boston: Houghton Mifflin Co., 1960). The concept of mental age is intended to help us understand the intellectual abilities or capacity of an individual, but a word of caution is needed. Terman and Merrill suggest that a person's mental capacity reaches its maximum by the age of eighteen years. This does not imply that he ceases to learn or to profit from experience. A person with a mental age of nine may not make much academic progress beyond that expected of the average nine-year-old, but he can continue to acquire additional knowledge and new skills. Most of us have our strengths and our weaknesses. Many persons who are mentally handicapped experience their greatest difficulty in the areas involving language and abstract reasoning, but they have relatively less difficulty in the "performance" or "concrete" areas.

As we have stated before, the outstanding characteristic of this group of children is their limited mental ability. They cannot learn as rapidly or comprehend as difficult and complex situations as can those of greater mental ability. If undesirable behavior is observed, it is often the result of the interaction between their limited abilities and the pressures and demands placed upon them by a society that does not understand.

Mentally Retarded-Trainable

About 0.5 per cent of our school-age children will develop at about half the rate of the normal child, or slower. These make up the semidependent group and are referred to as "trainable."

Mentally Retarded-Custodial

About one out of every 1,000 children is so severely retarded as to remain dependent throughout his life.

Neither the mentally retarded-trainable nor -custodial group is considered educable; that is, they will not be expected to profit from an academic program. The trainable group will have a maximum mental development of from five to nine years. The custodial group will not pass the five-year developmental level.

With other mentally exceptional groups we have stressed their physical similarity to the average child. Many people think of cretins, mongoloids, hydrocephalics, and microcephalics whenever mental retardation is mentioned. As a matter of fact, most of these clinical types that have marked physical differences are found in the groups under discussion (i.e., the—trainable and—custodial).

Problems. Frequently there are physical and psychological characteristics that create complex problems. Many of the trainable group can learn self-care and develop acceptable

40

social behavior. They do not have the judgment to make important decisions wisely. They may be taught good grooming, good manners, rules of safety, and to read a limited functional vocabulary (stop, go, ladies, gentlemen, entrance, exit, and so forth). The most able of this group will probably not learn to read above a third-grade level. Very close supervision of activities will be necessary. For the most part, their economic usefulness is limited to helping with simple tasks in their homes, although a few may be able to function in a sheltered workshop. At the lower extreme of the trainable group are those who (at home or in resident centers) must have the care and attention given to infants. Programs must be realistically planned, with the abilities of the pupils in mind. Those in the custodial group will always require the care given to infants or very young children.

Conclusions

As we close our discussion of the intellectually exceptional child, it may be wise to remind ourselves that the distribution of intelligence is continuous—that is, there are no chasms between the groups. The grouping may be necessary for administrative purposes, but the difference between the abilities of a child with an I.Q. of 79 and a child with an I.Q. of 81 is negligible—even though one may be eligible for special class placement under legislative provisions, while the other remains in the regular classroom.

We should also remember that intelligence is composed of many factors. Even the best intelligence tests do not purport to measure all factors. Of those that are measured, a child may be relatively weaker in the so-called "verbal" areas emphasized in the work of the schools and relatively stronger in the practical areas of manipulating and dealing with concrete situations.

41

One final word of caution: intelligence is only one of the factors that determine a child's development. Aside from environmental factors, there are such imponderables as motivation, determination, persistence, and energy. Physical and emotional problems may prevent a child from using the ability he has. Psychologists and religious leaders state that none of us use more than a fraction of our potential. Some of the mentally handicapped will not use all of their abilities. On the other hand, some will surpass our expectations, which, I suppose, reminds us that there is a great deal we do not yet know about the mind and the spirit of man.

2. IMPAIRED HEARING

IN THE area of impaired hearing the terminology is almost as confused and confusing as it is in the area of mental retardation. We shall use the terms as indicated below, though they are not given the same definitions by all writers.

Deaf: Those with hearing so severely impaired that they did not learn speech and language in the normal fashion. They were born deaf, or lost their hearing before acquiring speech.

Deafened: Those who had hearing adequate for learning speech and language in the normal fashion, but who later suffered such impairment of hearing that it is no longer functional for communication even with the amplification of a hearing aid.

Hard of hearing: Those whose hearing is impaired but is adequate for learning speech and language "through the ear," including those who need to use some type of hearing aid.

Incidence. About 0.5 per cent of our children of school age are deaf or deafened, and about 3 per cent are hard of hearing. Age, industrial noise, disease, and accident take their toll, so that the incidence of both deafened and hard of hearing persons is considerably higher for the total population than the figures suggested above.

The Deaf Person

Individuals in this group will differ, even though the "label" is the same. One deaf person may have considerable residual hearing, another have none. Other differences result from inherited characteristics, environmental variations, and the age of onset (the age at which the loss was incurred).

Deaf persons, compared to hearing persons, seem to be a little lacking in emotional stability and find adjustment to their environment a little more difficult. They do not appear to have more behavior problems. There seems to be as wide a variety of personality traits among deaf persons as is found among hearing persons.

The range of intelligence among deaf persons is about the same as among hearing individuals. Educationally, however, the deaf child is (on the average) retarded from one to three years.

Further reference will be made to the characteristics of the deaf person in the discussion of the person who is deafened.

Problems. Language is our principal avenue of learning and our most important tool for effecting adjustment in our constantly changing environment. Normally a child learns to understand voice and inflection before he understands spoken words. He understands spoken words long before he uses his first spoken word. He has quite a vocabulary before he begins to read or write. For the child who is deaf, this whole process is disrupted. It would be most surprising if the disruption of so important a process did not have some far-reaching effects.

Since speech is learned primarily "through the ear," the child who is born deaf will not learn to talk unless

43

specialized techniques are used. Even after he has pains-takingly been taught to pronounce a word, the deaf child will have difficulty in mastering the rhythm and phrasing of speech. He will also have difficulty in controlling the volume, pitch, and quality of his voice, for he cannot monitor his speech as does the hearing person. He can judge how it sounds only by the way it feels. Some deaf persons do an amazing job of learning to express them-selves through speech and learning to understand speech through lip reading (which is referred to by many writers as speech reading). However, many deaf persons who have spent years learning to talk find that they can communicate only with their immediate families and, perhaps, with a small circle of intimate friends. With their deaf friends they use the "manual language" of gestures or signs. This manual language may not lend itself to the expression of abstractions and subtle shades of meaning, but it is rapid and direct. It has been referred to as "the mother tongue of the deaf."

The deaf person has all of the needs of the hearing person, plus some specialized needs that result from his lack of or difficulty with communication.

The Deafened Person

Persons who are deafened present the same array of variable characteristics found in the hearing population. The disease or accident that causes the deafness may also cause physical or mental impairment, but this is not always the case. The child who is deafened is often somewhat retarded educationally, but not as much as the child who is deaf. The explanation may lie in the fact that, by definition, the deafened child had a foundation in language concepts and speech before he lost his hearing.

On the other hand, the deafened person has a problem of adjustment that the person born deaf never faces. The person born deaf grows up in a relatively silent world. He is handicapped, but he does not experience a sense of acute loss. The deafened person has the advantage of speech (which will deteriorate if steps to preserve it are not taken), but he experiences a keen sense of loss, for he can no longer understand speech or participate in activities and associations that require hearing.

Those who are deaf or deafened may tend to be a little more fearful and suspicious than the average person. This we will explore in the next section.

Problems. In addition to the problems of communication already discussed, the person who is deafened has a unique problem of adjustment. He cannot hear speech and is thus handicapped in the field of communication. He cannot hear warning sounds—the doorbell, the fire siren, the buzz of a bee. But the biggest psychological problem is encountered at a third level, or area, of hearing that we may think of as "connecting," or "primitive." This level includes all of the sounds that we hear but are consciously aware of only occasionally—the sound of distant traffic, the rustling of leaves, the vague sounds of movement in other parts of the house. These sounds furnish an auditory background for living. Their absence gives the person who is deafened a feeling of being separated from the living world. Never having been consciously aware of these sounds, he is depressed by their absence and does not know why. A long step is taken toward the reduction of this feeling of depression and separation when those who are deafened have been helped to an understanding of its cause. In their efforts to compensate for the loss of contact with a living world, some deafened persons resort to continuous muscular activity. It is as though, lacking auditory contact with the living world, they substitute movement as a means of keeping in touch with the world and assuring themselves that they are alive. It is helpful if this movement can be directed into recreational or creative activities.

If the adult (or child) is well adjusted before he becomes deafened, he has a better chance of maintaining good adjustment. If he has personality deviations before becoming deafened, the loss of hearing may tend to intensify them. Most of us are a little sensitive at some points and, at times, a little suspicious. We react as though a criticism of "my" hat were a criticism of "me." We are a little uneasy or suspicious if we hear our name spoken, or if conversation stops when we join a group. Most of us do a pretty good job of keeping our sensitivity and our suspiciousness under control. But the person who is deaf or deafened has many more of these experiences and finds it more difficult to control these unhealthy reactions.

We suggested above that the aimless, continual movement acquired by some persons who are deafened might desirably be directed into recreational or creative activity. Encouraging the deaf and deafened person to develop avocations helps him to fill his leisure hours and to establish contact with others who have similar interests. For all of us, time drags when we are idle. Those of us who hear, but have not developed the ability to enjoy solitude, tend to fill our idle hours with casual talk. The person who is deaf or deafened may lose himself in a gulf of self-pity unless he is encouraged to develop a variety of interests. Painting, writing, building models of all kinds, repairing electrical appliances, refinishing furniture, quilting—these and many other activities should be considered. Nor should we overlook the preparation of bulletins, addressing of mailing lists, and other church-centered activities which persons who are deaf can perform. These services are needed by the church; they are needed by the deaf person to help him keep in touch with the church and to know the joy of contributing.

The Person Who Is Hard of Hearing

Various studies indicate that, as a group, the child who is hard of hearing is not markedly different from the hearing child. As the degree of loss increases, however, the differences become clearer. The child who is hard of hearing receives somewhat lower scores on tests of intelligence than do his hearing peers. In performance or non-language areas the difference is negligible. In language areas the differences are greater. Admittedly, the difference indicated by the verbal tests may be a reflection of the hearing loss and the accompanying language deficiency rather than the result of a real difference in intellectual abilities.

Educationally, the child who is hard of hearing tends to be somewhat retarded, and the percentage of children with hearing handicaps who repeat grades is higher than the percentage of "normal" hearing children. Here again the chief difficulty seems to be with language skills.

Some studies indicate that, compared to hearing children of the same age, children who are hard of hearing tend to be less stable emotionally. We will explore this further in discussing the problems of the person who is hard of hearing.

Problems. This is not the place to enter into a discussion of "how we hear" or "types of hearing loss." It is necessary only to point out that various types of hearing loss affect speech and communication in different ways.

You have heard a person say, "Speak a little louder." You did, and the person said, "You don't need to shout. I'm not deaf." The person wasn't trying to be difficult. He was experiencing a phenomenon called "recruitment." With recruitment, a person may not hear ordinary conversation, but loud sounds seem as loud to him as they do to a person with normal hearing. It is easy to see that such a person would find it difficult to use a hearing aid. By the time he increases the volume so that he can hear, the sound suddenly becomes too loud for comfort.

With a "flat loss" a person may hear speech, but it sounds faint and far away. If speech is loud enough, it is heard and understood. If a child has a "flat" hearing loss, parents are apt to discover it at an early age. They discover that the child does not respond to sounds that are normally heard. Sometimes, however, they think he is disobedient or stubborn. One mother said, "He won't do a thing until I yell at him." His teacher said, "He's lazy. If I stand right over him he does what I tell him to do." Both were distressed to learn that they had misjudged the child; he had a hearing loss. Some parents use simple tests of their own. One mother spoke quietly from the next room, "Johnnie, here's a cookie for you." She had to speak with unusual volume before Johnnie answered and came hurrying out to claim the cookie. Professional testing revealed a moderate hearing loss.

A "regional" loss is more difficult for parents to detect. The child may hear enough speech at the normal level of intensity to respond to it, but not hearing the consonant sounds he does not use them. If you say, "Put the cat out, Dickie," he may hear "U uh a ou, i-ee." Not hearing the consonant sounds, he does not learn to use them.

Any type of hearing loss is likely to have its effect on speech. Voices may be too loud or too weak, pitch may be monotonous or lacking in expression; and articulation may be so defective as to make speech unintelligible.

With a child who is hard of hearing, as with the child who is mentally handicapped, many of the behavior problems are not the result of the impairment so much as they are the result of the unreasonable demands and pressures put upon the child. A child scolded for not answering when he did not hear you call must get the idea that this is an unreasonable world. A child who hears the shouted "No! No!" or "Stop that!" but never hears the softly spoken words of praise and endearment may be expected to have some problems of adjustment. Imagine the bewilderment and uncertainty of the girl who looks up when everyone laughs, but didn't hear the amusing comment; or the resentment of the boy who is accused of cheating because he continued to work on his test after the teacher said, "Time." Adults who are hard of hearing experience many frustrating and embarrassing situations. It is not surprising that some persons who are hard of hearing become overly aggressive, striking out in the only way they know at an environment that is unreasonable. Others tend to withdraw from the unfair competition and try to avoid any situation that holds the threat of humiliation or ridicule.

Many persons who are hard of hearing will need help in making satisfactory adjustments. Many of them will need hearing aids (either an individual type to be worn all the time, or a desk type to be used in the classroom or at home). Most of them will need help in developing adequate speech patterns. All persons who are hard of hearing should be taught speech reading to supplement their hearing. All of them need a climate of acceptance and understanding.

Through the use of hearing aids and special training, young children are able to overcome many of the problems caused by loss of hearing.

Suggestions. Many persons with impaired hearing are labeled stupid, stubborn, unco-operative, lazy, disinterested, or overbearing by those who do not know that these persons cannot hear. Recently two interesting instances of this sort came to my attention. A boy who had repeated the first grade was to be retained a third year because "he just wasn't ready for the second grade." Testing revealed normal intelligence and a loss of hearing. A teacher's dismissal was being urged by some parents because she "yells at the children and keeps them upset." Testing revealed a hearing loss. The first suggestion then, is be alert to the symptoms of impaired hearing.

49

Persons with defects of hearing may show one or more of the following symptoms: difficulty in locating the source of a sound; a voice that is too weak, too loud, or lacking in normal pleasant inflections; faulty equilibrium (particularly in the dark or when blindfolded); irrelevant answers or mistakes in carrying out directions; repeated earache or ear discharge; frequent requests for repetition of what has been said; peculiar listening posture (such as turning the head); anxious or listless expression (depending upon the temperament). If a hearing test administered by a qualified person (such as an audiologist, a speech correctionist, or a public health nurse) verifies the suspicion of hearing loss, the person should be referred to an otologist or ear specialist. The doctor may recommend medical or surgical treatment, or he may indicate the need for a hearing aid and lessons in speech reading.

Here are additional suggestions that are usually helpful for a teacher:

1. Your face should be visible at all times when you are talking to a person with hearing difficulties. Most persons who are hard of hearing do some speech reading (or lip reading) whether or not they are aware of it. They must see your face. Stand away from windows, so that the light is on your face rather than in the eyes of the person. Don't talk while writing on a chalkboard. Don't hide your mouth behind your hand or a book. Do your teaching and give instructions from a spot in the room that is advantageous for the person who is hard of hearing. If you walk around while talking, you make it more difficult for him to understand you.

2. Give the person with a hearing handicap preferred seating. He should be seated toward the front of the room, but not so close to you that he has to look up at your chin rather than at your lips. In a circle or around a table, he should be across from you. If you move the "teaching center," he should be encouraged to move his seat to a vantage point.

3. Use your best speech, but be natural. Exaggerated mouth movements and extra loud voice may be more confusing than helpful. Try looking in a mirror while you talk. If you talk with a "tight jaw" or with restricted movements of the lips, no speech reader can understand you. Use good articulation, and encourage others to do so. If a question is asked or a statement made in such a manner that you do not think the person who is hard of hearing can understand it, repeat the question or summarize the statement. (Good discussion leaders make this a practice for any audience!)

4. Many words sound alike (such as *red* and *read*); this is confusing enough, but, in addition, many words that do not *sound* alike *look* alike on the lips when they are spoken. The words *mad, bad, pad, mat, bat, pat, man, ban,* and *pan* all *look alike!* So do *nibble, nipple,* and *nimble.* Words that look alike are called homophenes, or homophenous words. There are many of them. No wonder the lip reader becomes confused! Encourage the person to ask for clarification when it is needed. In repeating an idea, it is often helpful to use different words. For example, "half a dollar" is much easier to lip read than "fifty cents."

5. Names of persons and places are particularly difficult. It will be helpful if they are written on the chalkboard. Key words for the discussion or the lesson outline may also be written. (The whole class will probably benefit.) If a list of names and unusual words to be used in next Sunday's lesson is sent home, the parent may help by familiarizing the child with them.

6. Try to help the person (adult or child) who has a hearing loss to develop a sense of humor. Help him to see the humor in his mistakes and to laugh at them. He needs to understand that he will make mistakes that are amusing. "Wash the baby" and "watch the baby" *look* alike, but the activities are quite different. He must understand that we are not laughing *at* him, rather we are laughing *with* him at the humor involved.

51

3. IMPAIRED VISION

THERE is no sharp line of demarcation between those who are "blind," "partially sighted," or "sighted." Vision specialists and educators have worked at forming definitions, but so far none has been universally accepted.

We are familiar with the term "20/20 vision" and probably know this means that at a distance of twenty feet a person can read the print that the person with normal vision can read at twenty feet. If vision is 20/70, the individual, twenty feet away from the chart, can read print no smaller than that which the person with normal vision can read at seventy feet.

Blind: A person whose vision in the better eye, using the best possible correcting glasses, is less than 20/200 is considered to be legally blind. We should note that a person may be legally blind and still have considerable vision. A person whose vision is 20/200 might read the headlines of newspapers. With 10/200 vision he could not read the headlines. With 5/200 vision he could perceive movement in objects nearby, but probably could not count fingers at a distance of three feet. With 2/200 vision, movement could not be perceived at distances of more than three feet, but discrimination between light and dark is possible. The person who is totally blind is not able to perceive light. In any event, a person is "educationally blind" if he cannot use his eyes as a primary avenue of learning.

Partially Sighted: Some writers use the term *visually handicapped* to refer to this group. These persons have seriously impaired vision, but with proper equipment and aids, they will be able to use their eyes as a principal channel of learning.

It is difficult to write definitions that take into consideration the many abnormal conditions that may seriously interfere with vision. Because of the presence of other factors (such as extremely limited visual field or improper focus at close range) a person whose vision is better than 20/200 may sometimes be thought of as "educationally blind," and a person whose vision is better than 20/70 may sometimes be considered (for educational purposes) to be "partially sighted."

Incidence. Because of differences in definition and variations in securing information, the precise number of blind children or adults in our country is not known. Some writers estimate that 20 per cent of our school children have visual defects that may be corrected by glasses; 0.6 per cent are partially sighted, and 0.1 per cent are blind.

Blind

Persons who are blind exhibit the same range of intelligence as do their sighted peers. Some studies suggest that the percentage of slow learners and mentally handicapped is somewhat higher among the blind than among the sighted, but this may be influenced by the blind person's limited experience and lack of opportunity to learn.

Educationally, the blind child is, on the average, somewhat retarded. One of the chief causes for this retardation is probably the relative slowness of reading Braille. Although some blind persons read Braille "surprisingly fast," the Braille reading rates are usually only one third to one half as fast as the rate at which persons with normal vision read.

Information concerning the personalities of persons who are blind is scant. What little data we have suggests that blind children are, on the average, more maladjusted than sighted children, and that blind girls tend to be more maladjusted than blind boys. Our discussion of the problems of persons who are blind will help us to understand some of their difficulties of adjusting to a sighted society.

Problems. It is obvious that a wide variety of problems will exist on the basis of differences in visual acuity among persons classified as blind. Add to this variable such factors

53

as intelligence and personality, and it is immediately apparent that no dogmatic set of rules can be laid down governing the education of blind children or adults. Their problems are not precisely the same. The following discussion, however, should be helpful.

Lacking sight, a person must rely on touch for actual knowledge of the physical world—the world of objects. The horizon of the blind person is limited to his arms' reach. Many things can be "seen" only through the verbal description given by others. Mountains, the Grand Canyon, the impressive Lincoln Memorial—these are too large to be perceived by touch. A snowflake, a dew-bedecked spider's web, a butterfly—these are too delicate to be perceived by touch. Flames, burning coals, boiling water, clouds billowing, objects in motion—these cannot be perceived by touch. The person who is blind must depend upon verbal communication, and this can neither effectively nor efficiently take the place of sight.

A child born blind learns the phrases "green as grass," "sky blue," "snow white," "blood red"—but they are only words. He has never experienced color. Do you understand how impossible it is for the blind person to "see" the world as we see it?

Facial expressions are, in part, a matter of imitation. Since the blind person cannot see the facial expression of others, he has less facial expression than the sighted person, and sometimes has a "silly grin" or "foolish grimace" instead of a "conventional" smile. Understanding *why* should make it easier for us to accept these differences in facial expression.

Have you been startled by a menacing growl or the caress of a cold muzzle when you did not know a dog was near? Experiences such as these happen frequently to a person who is blind. Spiders and snakes are among the many things that make no sound. Wind, rain, or confusion may drown out sounds that otherwise would be meaningful to the blind person and help him to keep aware of changes in his environment. People may enter or leave the room without being heard. Frequently the blind person cannot tell if the spoken "hello," "look out!" or "sit over here," is addressed to him or to someone else. There must, inevitably, be an increase in nervous tension and a feeling of insecurity.

To say that the person who is blind develops a "sixth sense" is to do him an injustice. His ability to interpret what is going on around him is the result of attention, practice, and the more effective use of his remaining faculties. There is no automatic increase in the acuity of other senses when a person loses his sight. He must concentrate. He must remember. He must learn to be aware of and to respond to cues of temperature, pressure, and pitch that are ignored by those of us who do not feel the need of them. "Facial vision" or the "sense of obstacles" with which the blind person is commonly credited, according to research studies, depends upon his sensitivity to the cues mentioned above and his ability to interpret them.[3]

The problems of the person who has been blind since birth are not quite the same as those of a child or adult who is becoming or has recently become blind. The person born blind is handicapped, but he experiences no acute sense of loss. He learns to read Braille as *the* way to read. The person who loses his sight has a problem of adjustment. He can no longer read swiftly—he must learn the slower method of Braille. We need not elaborate on the many other adjustments that are necessary, nor the long period of training and self-discipline required to learn how to use the minimal cues discussed above. It is not easy!

Young blind children can be taught to walk and move freely. The older a person is when his sight is lost, the more difficult it is for him to learn to move confidently. A cane or a guide dog helps the person who is blind to find an obstacle-free course, but the problem of orientation must

[3] Rudolf Pintner, Jon Eisenson, and Mildred Stanton; *The Psychology of the Physically Handicapped* (New York: F. S. Crofts & Co., 1941), pp. 231-33.

be solved for himself, unless he relies upon human assistance. To keep himself oriented, the person who is blind must keep in mind a "mental map." He must also keep himself located on that map. He relies upon the odors of the grocery store and the leather goods store, the air currents indicating a vacant lot or an alley, the slope of the sidewalk, the height of the curb. He also uses his sense of time and his "muscular memory." On our own stairway we know when we have reached the top step without either counting or looking—our muscles "remember."

This explanation is, obviously, an over-simplification. The point to remember is that the person who is blind must learn to interpret slight cues that most of us ignore; he must remember many details that the sighted person does not need; he must always be alert to detect changes in his environment—changes that the sighted person casually observes. And, in spite of his best efforts he can hardly be expected to adjust as completely or as easily as sighted persons do.

The environment of the person whose sight is impaired or lost must be brought within arm's reach.

Some General Suggestions. The horizon of the person who is blind extends only to the fingers of his outstretched arm. His environment should be brought within arm's reach as much as possible. Rather than pictures, objects and relief maps should be used. I have a blind friend who appreciates having his fingers guided over a road map so that he gets an idea of the location of landmarks, points of interest, and our destination.

Sufficient time must be allowed for introducing new projects so that the person who is blind can become properly oriented. The presentation of material should be well organized. This is good advice for any presentation, but it is essential when teaching or explaining to persons who are blind. Explanations must be specific and clear.

Speaking or reading aloud whatever is written on the chalkboard helps the sighted pupil, but is obligatory when a blind pupil is in the class. A sighted person may be assigned as the blind person's helper. The person who is blind must feel free to ask for help, and should be taught to accept help gracefully when it is needed. He should also be taught to refuse graciously when help is not needed. (This problem of graciously accepting or refusing help is faced by persons with all types of handicaps. It is especially difficult for those who have formerly known independence.)

Whenever a trip is planned, it is a good teaching technique to explain where you are going, what you are going to do, what you will see, and what safety practices are to be observed. This sort of preparation is even more important to the person who is blind. By anticipating situations that might be difficult and preparing for them, we help him to meet them with increased confidence.

The worship service will be more meaningful if persons who are blind or partially sighted are taken on a tour of the church when they may take time to "see" the carving of the pulpit; walk the width and length of the sanctuary; meet one of the ushers and accompany him down the aisle as he says, "We walk down the aisle like this. We stand here for the offertory prayer. The offering plates are placed here on the altar." Let them meet the organist and "see" the organ, sit in the choir seats, stand at the lectern, cross to the pulpit. Help them visualize the pageantry and dramatic development of a well-planned worship service. (Adults as well as children, may appreciate such a tour.)

As with other types of exceptionalities, much of the accompanying handicaps of blindness result from the attitudes of others. Blind people who have been helped to achieve a good adjustment do not want pity. Some problems result from a lack of understanding and a feeling of self-consciousness or awkwardness on the part of their sighted friends.

Specific Suggestions. Here are some suggestions to help you understand and be more comfortable with those who are visually handicapped:

1. Talk in your normal voice and use your normal vocabulary. Unless the blind person is also hard of hearing, there is no need to talk louder. Use such words as "look" and "see" without embarrassment. Many persons who are blind say, "Let me see it," when they want you to hand them an object for examination. Comment on the flowers on the altar, the new choir robes, or the view from the window in the same way that you would to sighted friends.

2. In acting as a guide, let the blind person take your arm. You may let your elbow touch him or place his hand on your arm. For the first few times, to see how well he manages, you may warn him of the need to step up or down. Usually, by walking slightly ahead, your own movements will guide him, particularly if you hesitate slightly before taking a step up or down.

3. The person who is blind will seat himself if you will place his hand on the back of the chair. In the sanctuary, guide his hand to the back of the pew in front of him. In entering a car, place his hand on the door, and he will do the rest. (Just be sure there is nothing on the seat!)

4. Upon being introduced, if you want to shake hands, don't hesitate to take his hand—he cannot see you extend

yours, so he may not extend his. You will, of course, take his hand if he extends it.

5. Speak to the blind person as you enter or leave a room so that he knows of your presence or departure. Saying, "I'll take this chair by the window," or some such statement, will let him know where you are. When you sit beside a person who is blind, or speak to him in a group, it is wise to identify yourself by name unless you are positive that he will recognize your voice. (Many newcomers with good vision would appreciate this thoughtfulness too!)

6. If someone who is blind is a guest in your church or in your home, show him around much as you would any guest, but let him explore a bit. He will need to walk across the sanctuary or your living room to judge its size, feel the carving of the reredos or the texture of the draperies, and so forth. Neither a man nor a woman should feel any embarrassment in showing a guest of either sex who is blind to the rest room in the church or the bathroom in your home. "The lavatory is here. The toilet is here. The tissue is on your right. These are the guest towels." It is as simple as that. If there is a paper towel dispenser that requires pushing a button and turning a crank, be sure your guest knows how to operate it.

7. Doors should be either closed or wide open. Half-open doors constitute real hazards.

8. If your church has a buffet supper, ask your guest if he would prefer to be seated and let you bring him a plate of food or go to the serving table with you. If he prefers to have you bring a plate, ask if there is any food he does not eat. If he goes to the serving table with you, you may ask, "Would you like some of this pretty potato salad?" or "This chicken looks good. What's your favorite piece?"

9. After seating him at the table, it is helpful to locate things by reference to the face of a clock. "On the plate there are mashed potatoes at nine o'clock. At twelve o'clock are strips of buttered carrots." You may continue with, "From your plate, at about one o'clock is a glass of water.

That's it. At about ten o'clock is a tossed salad." Occasionally we offer to cut the meat for our blind friends. Usually, once orientated, they manage so well that we completely forget they are blind.

10. If possible, discuss in advance the arrangements of the Communion service with your friend who is blind. He may prefer that you guide his hand to the tray, or that you serve him. In your own home you may say, as you hand him a glass of water, "Here is a glass of water. You may like to put it on the little table beside you." Don't move the glass or any other object that he is using. Once having located it, he will expect it to be in the same place.

11. The rules of graciousness and thoughtfulness that apply to any guest apply to the person who is blind. Be natural. When in doubt, ask questions. He will be glad to tell you what would make him most comfortable, and both of you will be at ease.

There is no "rule of thumb" to guide us. The personality factors and abilities of blind persons have as wide a variation as is found among sighted persons. To teach them, to help them solve their problems, to meet their needs— these are our goals. The requirements are a genuine love of persons, a sympathetic but objective viewpoint, and an imaginative, creative approach.

The Partially Sighted

A wide variety of intellectual ability is found among the partially sighted persons, and there is just as wide a variety of temperament or personality. Physically, too, there is wide variation, although some studies show that persons who are visually handicapped tend to have more than their share of physical limitations. In some cases the cause of the impaired vision is the cause of the physical handicap.

One characteristic that this group of persons seem to have in common is a strong desire to learn what they want to know by using what vision they have. It is important, therefore, for those who work with partially sighted persons (1) to understand that the limitations of vision often result in misconceptions that must be corrected, and (2) to know what materials and equipment are suitable for use in their instruction.

Problems. In addition to the obvious problems of being unable to read small print or visually distinguish fine details, there is a problem in developing spatial relationships. A person who is partially sighted is limited in his perception of his environment—the objects within it and their relationship to the background. Concepts developed through casual daily experiences by the person with normal vision may be lacking or distorted for the person who is partially sighted. "The house across the street" is not perceived as a beautiful white cottage, with red roof, lace curtained windows, and colorful flower gardens. It is either a grey "blob" or a part of the unexplored horizon. The clock on the wall may be only the source of a rhythmic ticktock. The edge of the table may not be distinguished from the floor.

It is easy to see that the person with impaired vision will be less able to cope with the problems of everyday living. He has all the needs and problems of his sighted peer, but is less able to deal with some of them. An adequate program will place emphasis upon developing the best possible personal adjustment.

Suggestions. In regard to instructional materials, our discussion must be inadequate because of limited space. Most of the persons in the group we are considering will be able to read books printed in large type, such as those available from the sources listed in the Appendix. If hand-printed materials are to be prepared, cream-colored paper with nonglossy or matte finish, black India ink, and a No. 5 Speedball pen or equivalent should be used. Letters should be of uniform size, no larger than the child needs. (Usually ¼- to ⅜-inch is satisfactory.) As in this book, the letters of each word should be close together; the spaces between the words should be about the width of one letter. Phrases, words that "go together," should be on the same line, rather than "Be ye" on one line and "kind" on the next.

If the person is to write, he should be furnished with matte finish paper of cream or green tint, ruled with green ink. The lines should be 1/24-inch wide and 3/4-inch apart. If the paper is ruled on both sides, the lines on one side should register accurately with those on the other. A pencil that makes a clear, black line should be used. As with sighted children, the younger should be given larger sheets of paper, say 11 by 17 inches, ruled the long way; older children and adults may use sheets 8½ by 11 inches, ruled the long way.

Maps should be in bold, black outline, and bear only the essential labels. Such maps may be made by projecting a slide on a sheet of paper, or by using an opaque projector to furnish the enlarged picture of a map. The projected picture may be penciled in, then traced with India ink. (An opaque projector may often be found in the public schools; it is very simple to use.)

If additional copies of any material are needed, photostats can be made by a blueprint company, and many offices now have devices similar to the Photostat. A few inquiries in schools, the courthouse, or large offices should locate a duplicating device that will produce positive copies (black lines on white paper).

Some partially sighted persons will be able to read material written on a typewriter with large type. Schools often have typewriters with extra-large type, sometimes called primer type. It will be worth investigating.

Like most children, those with impaired vision enjoy singing. As songs become longer, so that it is difficult to learn them as they are sung in the church school, the words may be printed in letters large enough for the child to read, or they may be typed and sent home so that parents can help the child learn the words. One teacher tape-recorded the words and music, then loaned the tape recorder to the child for a week.

There are problems in working with persons who have visual disabilities, but solving our problems with ingenuity is a most satisfying experience!

4. THE CRIPPLED PERSON

ALTHOUGH there is no definition of *crippled* that is universally accepted, a very simple statement will suffice for our purposes. We may think of the crippled person as one who cannot compete in physical activities with a normal individual of the same age. In the orthopedic sense, this includes those who, because of congenital or acquired defects, do not have normal functioning of the muscles, joints, or bones. Also included are those with chronic medical problems that interfere with or limit their physical activities.

Incidence. The number of crippled children and adults will, of course, vary from community to community. Various surveys report from six to thirty per thousand in our population. The chances are that you will find more males than females in this group.

Characteristics and Problems. The intellectual abilities of those in this group range from that of the mentally retarded to the gifted. There is some tendency for the person who is more severely crippled to be increasingly limited in intelligence, according to some studies. Unless we have the results of adequate objective testing, we will want to give a person the benefit of doubt, but will not want to add to his frustration by setting goals that are beyond his ability. At the same time, we must encourage him to explore his abilities—to do the things he is capable of doing. We are again reminded of the necessity for considering the individual needs and abilities of each person.

Educationally, the crippled child may be somewhat retarded. He may be working below his expected grade level because of extended confinement in a hospital, inability to carry a "full load" of academic work, mental retardation, or because of the interference with learning that results from inadequate control of the movements of hands and eyes.

Although we should emphasize the point that maladjustment does not inevitably result from crippling, it does not require much imagination to anticipate that the crippled person will have more problems than the physically able. He cannot walk as rapidly as others, he cannot climb stairs easily—and we find it difficult to disguise our impatience. Add to this the frustration of not being able to join in the activities shared by others. His life is filled with events which he may only observe, with no hope of sharing.

Nor is this all. People about him react to any physical deviation. Rejection, amusement, pseudo pity have not entirely disappeared. Furthermore, as he grows older, the crippled person becomes increasingly aware of the gap between his aspirations and his abilities. No wonder he has adjustment problems!

Crippling conditions are so numerous and varied that our space does not permit listing all of them. We are limited to brief comments concerning a few problems that may be particularly pertinent to our work in the church.

Cerebral Palsy

Cerebral palsy is a complex neuromuscular disability that results from a defect or damage of the central nervous system. Sometimes these persons are included in the group called "brain injured." Cerebral palsy has many forms and may affect only a few muscles or many. Some persons with cerebral palsy have great difficulty with movements because the opposing muscles seem to be fighting each other. Others cannot prevent involuntary movements of the hands, arms, legs, head, or mouth—they writhe with uncontrolled movement. A less common type of this disorder is characterized by a lack of balance and poor spatial conceptions. Still others in this group have small rhythmic movements or tremors; a shaking which they cannot control.

Impairment of hearing and some reduction in intelligence are often, but not always, present. Reading, writing, talking, and other activities that require fine muscular coordination present special problems for this group. For some of these persons, turning a page is a far greater victory than the seventy-five-yard run made by a brother in Saturday's football game. The expenditure of energy is enormous!

The inaccurate and difficult movements of limbs, eyes, and tongue slow down learning and make it impossible for the person to readily express in words or in writing what he does know. As a result, many persons with cerebral palsy actually function at a level considerably below their intellectual potential.

Add to all of these problems the frustrations encountered in interpersonal relationships, and it is easy to understand why some studies indicate that many cerebral palsied persons have serious emotional and social problems.

Brain Injury

The term "brain injured" is sometimes used to include the celebral palsied person, but it is a broader term, including other conditions that result from damage to the central nervous system. There is much we do not know about this poorly defined group. However, persons in this group may be expected to have some of the following characteristics: (1) Hyperactivity. The person cannot keep still. In so far as ingenuity permits, we should try to channel or direct the activity rather than forbid it. (2) Perseveration. Once a response (either verbal or muscular) has been made, there is a tendency toward repetition. The person may know that this is wrong or inappropriate, but he cannot prevent it. (3) Short attention span or inability to focus attention. (4) Confusion in trying to distinguish the details of objects and sounds from their accompanying backgrounds. A brain-injured person may be so intent on the sound of a distant siren or a cricket that he cannot hear your instructions; he may so concentrate on the background of a picture that he misses the central figure. (5) Overreaction. Most of us "screen" stimuli. We select the stimuli to which we will respond and ignore or devaluate others. With some brain-injured persons it is almost as though any stimulus had the power to touch off the utmost in response, no matter how inappropriate it may be.

All of these difficulties interfere both with learning and adjustment. Failure to understand the person's behavior results in additional problems. His conduct results in antagonism or ostracism by his peers. Adults punish the brain-injured child for behavior "he can't help." As a result, the limitations imposed by the brain damage itself are compounded by emotional problems that may include feelings of distrust, not being wanted, and general insecurity.

Poliomyelitis

In our rejoicing over the tremendous progress that has been made toward eradicating this infectious disease, we must not forget those who are handicapped because of it. The residual impairment may be limited (perhaps affecting only one arm) or widespread. If only limited impairment exists, it is generally thought that overprotection is one of the greatest dangers.

Not only is the person faced with the problems of adjustment involved in no longer being able to participate in many of the activities of his peers, he must learn to accept the fact that he will never again earn spending money by mowing lawns, or find peace and contentment in the smooth rhythm of skates on ice. This is bad enough. But how will he make a living? Will he marry and have a family? Most of us have a more or less realistic concept of self; if we are well-adjusted, happy individuals, we include in this concept our assets and our liabilities. The person recovering from poliomyelitis, like the person with the traumatic loss of limbs, sight, or hearing, must rebuild his self-concept. This is often a time of confusion and despair. The concept of self must be revised to include braces, wheel chair, and crutches. Later on, we will explore this aspect of the problem a bit further.

Other Crippling Conditions

Some persons have congenital amputations; that is, they were born with one or both arms or legs missing. Some have bones that are easily fractured. Some may have *spina bifida* —a lack of development in the vertebral column; these children usually have some impairment of the movement of the legs and there may be a lack of control of bladder and bowel.

Multiple sclerosis and muscular dystrophy are progressive diseases for which, at present, there is no cure. People in the early stages of these diseases offer the church school a real challenge. Can we help them to develop a faith, a philosophy of life that will enable them to face their future?

Some Generalizations. We have not exhausted the list, but no matter; for we are concerned with the individual, and each must be considered separately. We are, however, ready to make a few generalizations.

1. Not being able to do what others do (or, in cases of acquired defects, what they once did) creates problems of adjustment for persons who are crippled. These problems include a revision of self-concepts and life goals.

2. The reactions of others to their physical limitations often create additional problems. We are so aware of the braces or crutches, the drooling that results from difficulty in swallowing, the fingerlings on the stumps of arms, the

Too often we are so aware of the braces or crutches that we do not see the person.

bizarre movements of the cerebral palsied person—we are so aware of the handicap that we do not see the person. We react so violently to the handicap that we do not react to the person. Revulsion, rejection, pseudo pity, maudlin sympathy, overprotection—none of these is an appropriate reaction. None of them helps us in our avowed purpose of serving the needs of all persons.

3. Often, helping the person will involve helping his family. Some workers with handicapped children believe that the prime factor in the adjustment of the handicapped child is the attitude of his parents. Usually the problem of adjustment finds the child in the center of a complex situation that involves the entire family. A complete program must include help for the parents and for others whose lives are affected by the crippling condition. Irritations, frustrations, anxieties, rejection or overprotection—all play an important part in determining the attitudes, motivations, standard of values, and interests of the person who has the handicapping condition.

4. Many of the persons in this group are fearful of the very social relationships that they desire. They doubt their ability to measure up to expectations. They have met with rejection and condescension. Most of us have an urge to retaliate when we are criticized, especially if the criticism is unsolicited and, from our point of view, unwarranted or unfair. Some of these persons have an intensified need to retaliate. Even those who on the surface seem to have accepted and adjusted to their limitations may have hidden

68

fears and anxieties. In social situations that seem to them to be threatening or fearful, they may exhibit restlessness, irritability, or moodiness.

5. Sometimes both parents and child have strong guilt feelings. If a child has been required to spend long periods in a hospital, he may feel rejected by his family. Feelings of guilt and rejection may result in rebellion and resentment. The rebellion may take the form of withdrawal, nonconformity, or deliberate failure. On the other hand, the child may feel compelled to co-operate with adults, but will direct his hostility toward other children.

These are, admittedly, generalizations. There will be exceptions, and of course we will strive to understand the individual.

5. SPEECH HANDICAPS

QUITE a wide range of speech is considered normal. To be called "defective" the speech of the individual must be so different from the speech of others of the same age, sex, and community that it interferes with the two major purposes of speech. These purposes are (1) the communication of needs, ideas, and emotions, and (2) satisfying self-expression. Sometimes, even when the listener has no complaint, the speaker is so aware of a real or imagined difference that it causes him to be ill at ease, self-conscious, or maladjusted.

This is not the place to discuss the various types of speech problems. (There are many excellent books on speech correction and speech pathology that make interesting reading.) There are, however, a few points to be made here:

1. The sounds of speech are usually mastered by a child in a rather definite sequence. Several of the consonant sounds (including *s, r, th*) frequently are not mastered by a child before the age of seven and a half years. (Boys are usually slower than girls.)

2. By far the majority of children between the ages of

three and six or so have a period during which their speech is characterized by hesitations and repetitions—many of them. Part of the explanation probably lies in the fact that children of this age are encountering many new experiences and have neither the vocabulary nor the facility with grammar to express themselves. They need help—not criticism.

3. The large majority of speech problems are functional (that is, there is no physical abnormality sufficient to account for the defective speech), but some speech problems are caused by abnormal structure or functioning of the speech mechanism. It should be noted that chronic hoarseness is often the first indication of a pathological condition of the throat. To play safe with the child's health, any case of chronic hoarseness should be referred to a laryngologist.

4. The correction of even so-called "simple problems" may be complex, with emotional implications. It is wise to consult a professional speech correctionist.

Incidence. The remarkable fact is not that 10 per cent of our school children may be expected to have speech problems (and half of these will be quite serious), but that 90 per cent are able to master the complexities of speech without help. So complex is the business of speech correction that *no ethical therapist* will guarantee "a cure."

Problems. With the development of speech correction as a profession, our cultural attitudes have changed, but every person with a speech handicap knows that the old patterns of rejection and humor have not entirely disappeared. Any speech correctionist has heard such comments as these:

A CHILD: "I tried to get away, but they pushed me back and made me try to say things I can't say—and dirty words."

A UNIVERSITY ATHLETE: "I don't have any trouble getting the first date, but I never get the second. Girls can't stand the way I talk. The fellows aren't much better."

A HIGH-SCHOOL STUDENT: "I can't help it that I have no palate and talk through my nose. I feel like something unclean when people look away from me, but I'd rather be slapped than take their pitying glances."

Frequently, frustration and anxiety (resulting not so much from the speech handicap as from the reaction of others to it) create an emotional problem which more than doubles the handicap.

The psychology of the person with a speech defect is primarily the psychology of frustration. Impaired speech interferes with communication. Communication is the basic tool for adjustment. What could be more frustrating than something that consistently interferes with our human relationships? No wonder some studies indicate that the person with a speech defect tends to have a little more than his share of the undesirable personality traits that are present to some degree in most of us.

Many children with defective speech lack self-confidence. But such children are, first of all, children. They have all the reasons that others have for being unhappy, discouraged, shy, fearful—and because of the speech defect they are a little less able to deal with their problems.

Suggestions. It would seem that we could make two contributions toward helping the person with a speech defect. First, the teacher may follow the suggestions offered in Chapter II for building self-confidence. Second, we can create in our church school a climate that will make the person with a speech defect feel accepted and at ease, so that he will want to attend and will find self-realization in making his contribution to the group. This can be done by promoting an understanding of the problem and a Christian attitude toward it.

The first step toward dealing effectively in our church schools with a person who has a speech defect is to examine the teacher. In Chapter VIII we will give some attention to the qualifications and training desirable in a teacher, but right now we will stress just one point—she must be genuinely interested in people and accepting of them. This means two things: first, she will respect the individual personality of the person; and second, she will exhibit no reaction to his speech because she feels no reaction. This isn't as simple as it sounds. You see, it is not enough to *make up our minds* that we will be accepting—we must *be* accepting. It is not enough to *act* as though the lisping and stuttering or nasal voice doesn't bother us—it *must not bother us*. We must accept the whole person—speech defect and all. For the present, at least, this is the way he talks. For some reason, this is the best he can do—and it is good enough for us. We accept his way of talking and react to *what* he says, not to *how* he says it. If he answers correctly, he deserves to feel good about it. "That's fine," said sincerely by the teacher, reassures the child and makes him feel that the teacher approves of him. Furthermore, if the teacher accepts him and approves of him, the members of the class will tend to accept her evaluation—they, too, will tend to accept and approve. Such approval and acceptance is both good for the child and good for his speech.

Although there is much that parents or others can do to help a child improve his speech, it is desirable—perhaps essential—that the layman work in co-operation with, or at least under the guidance of, a professional speech therapist. If your community does not have the services of a speech therapist, you may want to work through the P.T.A. or the school board to try to stimulate interest in employing one. In most states, substantial financial aid is given to encourage local school districts to provide this service. Consult your state department of education.

6. THE EMOTIONALLY DISTURBED PERSON

OUR discussion in this section will be concerned primarily with children, not because there are no adults who are emotionally disturbed, but because we will probably find ourselves in a "teacher-pupil" relationship with children more frequently than with adults, and if we can help children with even minor problems we may reduce the number of adults who have major problems. On the other hand, much of what is written here has its application to adults who are in this category. As we change our own attitudes concerning psychiatrists, psychiatric social workers, and family counselors, it will be easier to get adults to seek the professional help that is needed both for themselves and for their children.

Definition. "Emotionally disturbed" and "socially maladjusted" are elastic terms that include a wide variety of problems and behavior patterns. If a person's behavior interferes with his personal growth and development, his learning, or the lives of others, we may consider him to be poorly adjusted or disturbed. We are not concerned in this section with the disturbances that are rather quickly relieved with a spoonful of sympathy. Almost every child fluctuates in his behavior. (Don't we all?) He may have an "off day" because his pet rabbit died, he is angry with a playmate, he is going (or can't go) to the circus tomorrow. At such times he may be sullen, aggressive, withdrawn, hyperactive, defiant, or easily discouraged. In fact, he may exhibit any of the characteristics that we associate with being maladjusted or disturbed.

As children grow and develop they have their problems— problems that may seem insignificant to the adult, but are overwhelming when tackled from the viewpoint and with the abilities of a child. Yet, if a child is basically secure, the "squalls" are weathered, the temporary disturbances are resolved, and the child returns to "normal." During these periods of stormy weather we will want to provide the sympathy, understanding, and support that will prevent what should be passing symptoms from becoming chronic or severe. We are concerned in this section with the child whose symptoms of maladjustment are chronic.

Incidence. The reported incidence of maladjusted or disturbed children varies from 3 per cent to 20 per cent of our school-age children. There are several explanations for the variations in estimates. For one thing, there is no definite "yardstick"—parents and teachers differ in their interpretation of terms used in any definition. Some studies report only the number of children who are receiving professional help with their problems. Still another factor is the tendency to overlook the withdrawn child—the child who is too passive, who is "never any trouble." Possibly the figure of 20 per cent represents the children who would profit from professional help, while a smaller percentage of children are critically in need of therapy.

We have a tendency to overlook the withdrawn child—the child who is too passive, who is "never any trouble."

Characteristics. Disturbed or maladjusted children may look like their peers and behave like them part of the time or in some situations. Any bit of behavior must be interpreted in relation to its entire setting. Let us consider a boy "who never plays with other children, but always hurries home after school to work alone building a model airplane." Is this avoidance of playmates a withdrawal from the world of reality? Is he antisocial? We must know more about the boy and the situation before we can reach a conclusion. Do his parents, for logical or illogical reasons, prohibit his playing with other children? Are there children in the neighborhood of an appropriate age for him to play with? Is he so retarded or so superior that he does not share the interests of neighborhood children? For that matter,

74

what is meant by "always"? Is this a passing interest in a new set of tools, or does he usually avoid other children? Is he hoping to enter the model plane in a contest in order to gain status in the group, or to earn a cash prize, or to please his father? It is impossible to interpret any bit of observed behavior in isolation. The total situation must be taken into account.

Maladjustments do not come to full bloom overnight. There are always distress signals—warning signs—but we do not always recognize them. Here again, a sympathetic observation of the child is needed to detect the signs of developing maladjustment. Not until he has been identified as needing help can any plans for effecting better adjustment be made.

Danger Signals

A discussion of neuroses, psychoneuroses, functional and organic problems is not needed here. They are the province of the professional worker. However, the danger signals to watch for include the following:

a) *Aggressiveness*
  (1) Gets angry frequently, fights often, is quarrelsome.
  (2) Usually disagrees with decisions made by the teacher or by the group.
  (3) Picks on or "bullies" other children.
  (4) Impudent, defiant, rude to adults.
  (5) Defies rules and regulations, defiant or sullen when corrected.
  (6) Steals, lies, is destructive of property.
  (7) Difficult to manage, disrupts class routine.
  (8) Irritates and annoys other children.
b) *Withdrawal*
  (1) "Too good"—always obedient, co-operative.
  (2) Always neat—can't get dirty, dislikes finger paints.

75

   (3) Often left out—not disliked, just not noticed by other children.
   (4) Daydreams a lot (may be called "lazy" or "inattentive").
   (5) Always gives in—never "stands up" for his rights or ideas.
   (6) Has his feelings hurt often and easily, is easily upset.
   (7) Gives up easily—is readily discouraged.
   (8) Reluctant to join group activities, is not at ease in the group.

c) *General*
   (1) Appears to be unhappy or sad much of the time.
   (2) Is excluded from group activities by other children.
   (3) Seems to be indifferent or inattentive (sometimes thought of as "lazy").
   (4) Needs frequent reminding, prodding, and encouraging to get his work done.
   (5) Fails in school or achieves much less than objective tests of his ability indicate that he should.
   (6) Is jealous or excessively competitive (just *must* win).
   (7) Is chronically anxious, tense, "out of sorts."
   (8) Has nervous mannerisms (bites nails, sucks thumb, has tics, scratches, picks, stutters, is extremely restless, twists clothing or hair, chews tie or collar).

One quarrel, one lie, one refusal to join the group is not sufficient basis for rushing a child to a guidance clinic. But if several of the descriptive terms listed above apply to a child, it is time to do something to help the situation—and to help the child.

There is no sharp line between what is considered "normal" and what is considered "maladjusted." Symptoms vary in degree from the child who seems to have a little more than his share of the normal variations of mood and behavior to the child whose behavior interferes with learning through extreme hostility and aggressiveness or extreme withdrawal.

Problems. Emotionally disturbed children are sick children. The more seriously ill should have the help of the best psychiatric or counseling service available. Furthermore, professional diagnosis must be had if we are to deal wisely with the illness.

People vary in their degree of awareness of their own maladjustment. Some are completely unaware that a problem exists. Some are vaguely aware that something is wrong, but do not dare admit their need of help. Others know that they have problems (but this is not the same as saying that they "understand" the problems). Still others, who may be thought of as exemplary by their teachers and envied by their classmates, are convinced that they have problems—even though no one else thinks they have. The problem may be an acute fear, a feeling of inadequacy in certain situations, or a general feeling of not being able to measure up to what is expected of them. For all of these, help is needed.

Understanding the disturbed child is not easy. We need the information and advice that only a psychiatrist or a child psychologist or a pediatrician with an adequate background in child psychology can give. In many cases it will be impossible to understand the person and his problem in the absence of professional diagnosis. This means that there is a tremendous need for patience and acceptance.

Suggestions. Because of the diversity of symptoms and causes, general suggestions for dealing with disturbed children will have only limited application for a particular child; however, the following may be helpful:

1. The disturbed child is an exceptional child. Because he is exceptional, the techniques that stimulate learning for most children may adversely affect the disturbed child. The teacher must be alert and sensitive to the responses of the child, and be ready to modify or abandon techniques or procedures that do not yield satisfactory results.

2. His problem is real. It is not fair to say that the disturbed child "could do the work if he wanted to." Whatever we call him—resistant, stubborn, negative, aggressive—the problem is as much beyond his control as defective vision and as real as a missing limb.

3. It is not personal. Don't think that the boy who continually disrupts the class, in spite of your efforts to be his friend and help him, has anything against you personally. The problem goes much deeper than that. He may want your friendship and approval more than anything else, but because of his problems he cannot conform.

4. He is trying. In many cases a child is not conscious of the real nature of his problem, but the behavior (of which we disapprove) may be for him a solution to some conflict. It may not be a happy or effective resolution of the problem, but it is the solution that he has found, and he will not readily abandon it.

5. Know the child. Accumulate all of the information that is available. Learn all you can about the child from his classroom teacher, the school psychologist, the public-health nurse, the parents. As you get a better understanding of his problem, as you come closer to the "why" of his behavior, you will become more accepting of him. Your new attitude may reduce the tensions and anxieties of the child. As you acquire increased sympathy for the child, you may need to guard against developing an antagonistic or overly critical attitude toward the parents. In most cases, the parents are doing what they rightly or wrongly believe is best for the child. In other cases they are doing the best that they can considering their own human limitations, backgrounds, and frustrations.

6. Individualize instruction. As you accumulate data about the child you will perhaps discover his learning ability. You may also learn that he responds particularly well in certain situations. You may find that he can deal fairly well with concrete situations, but is unable to deal with abstract concepts. The material you present must not only be

at the child's level of intellectual ability, it must be at his level of interest and sophistication. Sometimes a group project makes greater individualization of instruction possible.

7. Be prepared. You will want to plan your teaching goals and your methods of achieving them. But plans must be flexible. Children need a sense of accomplishment, but they tend to tire of a theme or a project rather quickly. The good teacher will be sensitive to the mood of the class and quick to capitalize on shifts of mood or interest.

8. This is normal: regression, outbursts of temper, periods of frustration, short attention span, days when nothing seems to hold their interest and everything goes wrong —these are to be expected. In a class of disturbed children all of these difficulties are accepted as "normal."

9. Be objective. You must genuinely *like* children, but you must avoid becoming emotionally involved if you are to meet their needs—which include stability and security. The good teacher will not be "on the defensive" when a child says, "I hate you 'cause you're mean." She will not be shocked by an outburst of profanity, or by references to sex. As the needs of the individuals require, she will be more permissive or more controlling, but she will not be vindictive or retaliatory.

10. Know your limitations. Do not confuse your role as teacher with that of psychotherapist. You will need all of the psychological background and insight that you can acquire, but you are not a therapist. Some of the mildly disturbed or maladjusted may improve dramatically as a result of your acceptance and understanding. But the more disturbed or maladjusted will require the skills and insights of the child psychologist or psychiatrist. If professional help is not available, we may want to start a movement that will establish at least a part-time child guidance clinic in the community.

11. Be observing! As you establish friendly relations with the children they will be apt to reveal some of their inner feelings through what they say or what they draw. You will

listen and accept, but you will not interpret. Sometimes letting a child talk about his feelings (or fears) to an accepting, unshocked adult is beneficial. But interpreting what he says (or draws) is dangerous for anyone but a psychiatrist! You will also listen to parents. From them you will increase your understanding of the child. But you will carefully refrain from giving advice. Too often the amateur help given only makes matters worse by increasing the anxiety of the parents or by building up greater problems for the child.

12. Seek help. You will want to be familiar with all of the services available in your community. Is there a child guidance clinic? a family service agency? What help is available through your state department of public health? State department of public instruction? The state's bureau for handicapped children? What diagnostic or clinical services are available in colleges or nearby communities? Since you are neither a diagnostician nor a therapist, you will want to know to whom parents may be referred and to whom you can turn for advice.

13. Know mental hygiene. You will want to learn all that you can about good mental health and practices that encourage it. With children who are sufficiently mature, you may want to have a unit in which you study mental health and problems of adjustment. Anything we can do to improve their mental health will help to alleviate their symptoms.

14. Neutralize the program. As teachers, we are accustomed to asking, "Will this be stimulating? Will it allow the children self-direction and expression?" For most emotionally disturbed children it may be wiser to ask, "Is this neutral?" Maladjusted children tend to interpret events, stories, and materials in terms of their problems. We can try to neutralize the program by choosing materials and methods that are not likely to arouse fantasies or disturbing feelings in the child—in other words, stay away from his "sore spots." (This, of course, requires knowing the child.) Teachers who have tried this approach report that the

materials least likely to be disturbing are: those that deal with distant (in time or space) characters and situations; struggles against nature (rather than interpersonal hostility); studies of nature or science, rather than stories of intimate family relationships.[4] Another factor in neutralizing the program is the teacher's unshocked, casual, matter-of-fact, unruffled approach to or handling of touchy issues.

15. Be patient. Changes of attitude are not made quickly. Behavior patterns that have been adopted as a solution to a conflict are not easily abandoned. We can expect regressions or "setbacks." We can expect progress to be slow. But if, with prayer and patience, we have done our best, we have the satisfaction of knowing that our church has reached out, accepted, and served another group of God's children.

7. THE MULTI-HANDICAPPED PERSON

Definition. A person who has more than one handicapping condition is referred to as multi-handicapped. Unless we have a thorough evaluation we are apt to see his more visible limitations and overlook other exceptionalities. Without being aware of all a person's characteristics, his strengths and his weaknesses, we cannot hope to plan a program of Christian education that will meet his needs. This is particularly true where the multi-handicapped person is involved.

Characteristics. Although there are no surveys that indicate the incidence of multi-handicapped persons, we know that speech problems are often found in children who are mentally retarded, but there are also a surprising number of gifted children who have speech handicaps. Those with a hearing loss often have speech problems. The cerebral

[4] Stanley Jacobson and Christopher Faegre, "Neutralization: A Tool for the Teacher of Disturbed Children," *Exceptional Children* (February, 1959), pp. 243-46.

81

palsied and the epileptic child, like others, may be mentally retarded. Emotional problems are found in combination with every kind of exceptionality. Mental retardation may be found in combination with all physical disabilities. You cannot imagine greater complications than are actually encountered. (Recently my colleagues and I were asked to recommend an educational program for a nine-year-old boy who is hard of hearing, has a severe speech problem, is partially sighted, seriously disturbed, and has a medical diagnosis of brain damage!) Since there is such a diversity of problems, it is impossible to give any description of the general characteristics of multi-handicapped persons. We must evaluate each individual. However, all such persons seem to have at least one thing in common—frustration. Counseling, guidance, and mental hygiene will be needed.

Problems. The persons of this group constitute a grave problem for those who are eager to provide the best possible opportunities in Christian education for all youth. The teacher who has acquired the special techniques necessary for teaching the child who is blind may not understand the problems of the child who is deaf. The teacher who is prepared to teach language to the child who is deaf may know little about the problems of the mentally retarded or cerebral palsied. True, all of these teachers have much in common—a love of people, an understanding of normal psychological and physical development, an ability to see the person beyond the exceptionality, and an acceptance of persons who are "different." They also have a respect for, but may have little understanding of, the fund of knowledge, methods, and materials of other "special" teachers.

Each multi-handicapped person must be studied and evaluated so that he may be given the best that our limited knowledge and facilities can provide in the church school. This is not a simple matter. As individuals we may be concerned with the total rehabilitation (or habilitation) of handicapped individuals. We will encourage research in this complex area and, in co-operation with our schools and other agencies, try to provide a complete program. In our church schools we will try to enroll a person (whether "normal," handicapped, or multi-handicapped) in a class and setting that will contribute most to the improvement of his social adjustment, broaden and deepen his sympathies, help him develop a Christian philosophy of life, and enable him to find his place in God's plan. In short, we will try to arrange for him to "grow in favor with God and man." He may need a ramp so that his wheel chair can be pushed into the church, a hearing aid so that he can take part in the class discussion, and specially prepared materials so that he can read them with his impaired vision. But whatever he needs in order to reap the maximum benefit from what the church school has to offer—this we will try to provide.

8. THE INSTITUTIONALIZED PERSON

SOME communities do not have the facilities that make it possible for a seriously handicapped person to live at home and receive the special help that he needs. Rural areas and small communities may not have enough deaf or blind children to make it economically feasible to organize a special class and employ an adequately prepared teacher in their public schools. The same situation exists with other areas of exceptionality. These children, in order to receive an education, must live in an institution or a boarding home in another community where facilities are available. There are both private and state supported schools for the blind, for the deaf, and for certain other exceptionalities.

In addition, there are institutions, schools, or treatment centers for those who are disturbed, or delinquent, or homeless. And, of course, there are our "boys' schools," "training schools," and "penal colonies" for those who, for a wide range of reasons and from a diversity of socioeconomic backgrounds, have been sentenced by the court.

Before we can serve we must understand. Something has

already been said of the characteristics of most of the exceptional types. Let us turn our attention now to those who are in prison, or in training, or reform, schools—those who have been labeled "delinquent" or "criminal."

Characteristics and Problems. As in most other groups, we find a staggering variety of problems and needs among so-called delinquents and criminals. For example, there are young persons and some adults in penal institutions because of one unfortunate, unwise, or rash act, who are "heartily sorry" for their wrongdoing. There are others alongside them who have faced judge and jury innumerable times— the so-called "hardened criminals." There are those who in a moment of overpowering temptation broke a law, and those who lack the capacity to "feel for others" and hence see nothing wrong with what they have done. There are well-educated professional people and those who had little or no education. There are those who were accustomed to "the good things of life," and those who have known nothing but poverty and want. There are those who have family and friends loyally waiting to help them find a place in society when they are released, and there are those who are convinced that no one cares what happens to them.

They are different—no two alike. Yet all are alike in their need for comfort, release from guilt, renewed strength, and renewed faith. In short, they need to have the gospel of Jesus Christ preached to them, demonstrated to them, and practiced on them.

9. THE HOMEBOUND PERSON

THE homebound, obviously, are the children and adults who, because of any one of a variety of reasons, are not able to leave their homes. Sometimes the person who is confined to his home because of some crippling condition causes one or more other persons to be "homebound" also, because he cannot be left alone. Sometimes there may be danger of infection or contagion, but the majority of those who are homebound pose no health problems to others. Tactful inquiry through your physician will answer questions regarding health.

Incidence. No figures are available as to the number of homebound persons you may expect to find in your community. However, two statements may safely be made. First, there are more people homebound than most of us are aware of. Second, some of them need not be homebound if proper transportation and motivation to leave home are provided.

Characteristics and Problems. With so diverse a group as this, no description of characteristics is possible. However, in addition to the characteristics discussed earlier in this chapter in sections that may be applicable to any individual, we may expect to find loneliness, devaluation of feelings of personal worth, and guilt feelings. ("Because of me, my family cannot do what they would like to do. I am guilty of depriving them.") Other members of the family may have attitudes of overprotection, rejection, or guilt feelings. ("In some way, I must be responsible for this condition. God is punishing me.") Sometimes the obvious overprotection is a cover-up for feelings of rejection. The emotional involvements may be quite complex. A person well trained in counseling and social work may be needed in some cases.

These are some of the persons in our community who have exceptional needs. Many of them are not now being reached by the church. Before we can serve them, we must find them. We will consider that problem in the next chapter.

CHAPTER IV

How Do We Find Them?

BEFORE WE CAN HELP PEOPLE WITH EXCEPTIONAL NEEDS WE must find them. Perhaps we should begin by admitting that we probably will not find many of these persons already in our church programs. The review of a few incidents will help us understand why.

The last time Julia was present the teacher asked her to repeat the sentence, *Jesus seeks a humble heart.* Julia looked puzzled because it really didn't seem to make sense, but she repeated what she had heard. "Jesus sneaked through Humboldt Park." The class laughed; Julia cried. Julia has a hearing loss.

Remember the young man who came in a wheel chair one Sunday? One of the men who helped to carry Jack and his chair up the steps said, "I'm glad your class isn't on the third floor!" Jack interpreted this as reluctance to help. Besides, that was the day you spent much of the time planning for a party. Jack was convinced that coming to church school had been a mistake. He didn't belong.

Tom has a cleft palate and talks with a high-pitched, nasal voice. The children laughed and called him "Squeaky." He never came back.

Of course, we have some exceptional persons in our church program, but we don't have all of those who need the church because we have not provided for them, and some who came did not feel welcome. If we are to serve them we must find them. How shall we go about it?

First of all, you can start where you are. If yours is a small church you may not have either the leadership or the workers required for an all-out community survey. But you can do something. You can make a study of the families in your church and neighborhood to discover persons who are exceptional. You can also find out what schools and other groups are working with exceptional persons and the types of assistance that are available. This information can then be used in developing your church's ministry to reach the exceptional persons you have discovered.

Values in a Survey

Where a more comprehensive survey is possible, it will be most helpful. You may want to start with your own congregation, or with the area served by your church. You may want to enlist other congregations in an interdenominational survey. Probably the most complete plan would be a community-wide self-appraisal. Such a comprehensive approach would have several advantages.

1. A community-wide survey will help create the attitudes toward exceptionalities that we must have if we are to serve exceptional needs.

2. Such a survey will make it easier to achieve the interdenominational co-operation that will probably be needed to achieve certain goals. It is possible that some churches will co-operate in a community project less reluctantly than they would co-operate with other denominations in a strictly church-centered project. This will serve to alert them to the various needs; and through the planning and evaluating sessions, they will be more likely to see the desirability of interdenominational sponsorship of a "special class," if the survey should indicate such a need.

3. We are interested in meeting all of the needs of exceptional persons. Particularly, we are concerned about the responsibility of the church, but as Christians we cannot stop there. A community self-appraisal may disclose the needs for special classes or specially trained teachers in our schools, a child guidance clinic, a family service agency, a sheltered workshop, a social worker on the educational

staff to serve as a liaison between schools and other agencies, a speech correctionist, more adequate recreational facilities. All of these and more may be indicated if the needs of all are to be met. Community interest and support will be needed.

4. A community-sponsored project will make it much easier to secure help from such sources as the state bureau for handicapped children (or similar division of your state department of public instruction), the state department of public welfare, state board of health, state agency for mental health (which may be under the department of health, welfare, or public instruction), local and state chapters of the Society for Crippled Children and Adults, colleges and universities with special education programs, and groups interested in mental retardation, cerebral palsy, or muscular dystrophy, to name only a few. Often the departments and groups listed above are able to lend professional members of their staffs to guide and counsel with the various committees. These professional workers will be able to suggest sources of information and assistance, help determine what data are needed, help interpret the data collected, help structure a program, and suggest methods of financing services that are needed.

5. Other advantages will occur to you in terms of your own community, but do not overlook the fact that having representatives of state agencies on your advisory or steering committee will help the community recognize the importance of the study.

How One County Did It

In April of 1954, Waukesha County, Wisconsin, undertook "An Appraisal of Community Services for Children and Youth." The Waukesha County Council of Social Agencies spearheaded the move to launch the survey. This council is composed of representatives of groups and agencies interested in social problems. They are so busy that they must hold their monthly council meetings at breakfast time. The survey was begun in October—the intervening six months being used to secure the co-operation of state and local groups, setup committees, and plan the work. One hundred ninety-four adults served on one or more of the eleven committees, and forty-one young persons attended at least three of the five meetings of the youth participation section. Actively co-operating were the Division of Children and Youth of the State Department of Public Welfare, the Division of Correction, Division of Mental Hygiene, Division of Public Assistance, State Board of Health, Wisconsin Free Library Commission, and the Wisconsin Welfare Council, in addition to various local professional groups.

In September of 1955, after eleven months of work, an eighty-three page report was issued. Local service clubs contributed funds to help defray the cost of printing.

Was all this worth the effort? The people who took part in it think so. Although the appraisal and recommendations were released five years ago, many of the goals have not been attained. This thorough appraisal served and continues to serve as the basis for long-range planning. Waukesha County (which adjoins Milwaukee County) is one of the fastest growing in the nation. Some of the recommendations must, of course, be modified. But the over-all outline is there!

We are members not only of *a* church—we are members of *the* Church. Our interests are universal. Most of us cannot serve personally in distant lands. We can serve in our own community. We recognize the fact that a "community whose agencies and citizen groups study their own problems, are alert to needs based on facts, and who take constructive steps to meet their needs, is in the strongest position to prevent serious problems among children and youth." [1] It is noteworthy that many of the recommendations made in the Waukesha appraisal "can be carried out without additional

[1] *An Appraisal of Community Services for Children and Youth in Waukesha County,* by Citizens of Waukesha County (Wisconsin: 1955), pp. 15-21, 31. Copies of this report not available for general distribution.

expenditure of funds or additional personnel. Some of them, if carried out, may result in savings of funds and all point to better services through better coordination." [2]

A few of the recommendations that are presented in this self-appraisal (quoted in full or in part) will suggest the scope of the study. It is obvious that the implementation of some of the suggestions that do not directly involve the church is necessary if the needs of youth are to be met. It is interesting to note that the first suggestion quoted below is the first to be found in the report:

> Churches and schools in local communities should work out plans for a designated day each week reserved for church activities.
>
> Churches should co-operate in a training program for adult leaders of youth groups. . . .
>
> Local law enforcement agencies should coordinate their work with juveniles more closely with that of the school authorities. . . .
>
> Recognizing the importance of early discovery of child adjustment problems . . . a qualified school social worker. . . .
>
> Youth serving agencies . . . a joint program for recruiting, training and giving recognition to adult volunteer youth leaders. . . .
>
> Additional personnel for the child guidance clinic. . . .
>
> . . . the needs of the aged. . . .
>
> . . . additional speech correctionists. . . .
>
> . . . visiting teacher. . . .
>
> More social programs for the entire family to be provided by the churches.
>
> Expansion of leisure time programs for youth. . . .
>
> More opportunities for youth participation in which youth develops its own program plans, works with adults . . . for community betterment. . . .
>
> Mental health and psychiatric services for adults.

---

[2] *Ibid.*

Agencies and organizations that offer family life education programs should continue, extend and publicize them. . . .

Clergymen should be better acquainted with the directory of health and welfare services . . . and joint meetings between members of ministerial groups and the council of social agencies . . . to exchange information about each other's services and programs. . . .

. . . public bathing beaches meet at least minimum public health standards. . . .

In the field of church-school relationships, the churches should recognize their limitations. Facilities, leadership, etc., are less professional, and the real merit of a spread-thin program poorly organized and led is questioned. On the other hand and just as firmly, the schools must also recognize the limitation of their program, and therefore recognize the limitation of their claim on the pupils. The Whole Man is not educated at school. One simple step in the right direction would be a "church nite" during the week respected by the school.[3]

There are many other suggestions, but these will serve to illustrate both the scope of the study and the manner in which these "community-wide" recommendations will supplement and augment the work of the church.

In order to plan wisely and to meet adequately the needs of all exceptional persons, we must know what services or special provisions are needed. We may not be able to provide immediately for all of the exceptional needs, but we can make our plans in such a way that additional services may be added as an integral part of the long-range program. Without such a master plan efforts are more likely to be sporadic, overlapping, and inadequate. The community self-appraisal will help provide this larger view.

Although local considerations will determine the approach best suited to your interests and your community,

[3] *Ibid.*

the following suggestions may at least serve as a springboard for developing your own plans.

Getting Organized

1. *Organization of a planning committee.*
   a) You may wish to start with members of your own congregation. The need for the survey should be explored and thoroughly understood.
   b) If an interdenominational survey is considered desirable, your minister may present the proposal at a meeting of the ministerial association, or some of your committee may be invited to meet with them. Each congregation should be represented on the planning committee. Again, the need for services to exceptional persons and for the survey must be discussed and understood.
   c) If the desire for a community self-appraisal develops, many other people and agencies must be involved; you will want representatives of the public schools, juvenile court, law-enforcement agencies, public health department, library, leisure-time and recreational agencies, and so forth.
2. *Duties of the planning committee.*
   a) Education. People will be more eager to work on the survey if they know enough about the problem to be interested. Suggestions for educating the congregation or the public will be found in Chapter V. The planning committee might wisely use some of these methods.
   b) Develop an over-all plan. The details of the planning should be left to the various committees, but the planning committee should formulate a general outline of the survey. Members may also prepare a statement of need and purpose, a list of committees (or areas to be covered), a list of co-operating groups and their representatives, and a list of groups whose sup-

A committee representing various community interests
and agencies—and if possible the various churches—
should plan the best way to collect and use the needed
data about exceptional persons in the community.

port should be enlisted. The committees might
include a steering committee and committees
on health, leisure-time services, family and children's agencies, financial and social planning,
law enforcement, juvenile court, library services,
church and family life, schools, and youth
participation. This last-named committee would
seek to provide an opportunity for representatives of youth groups to participate in the
survey, to study reports of committees that are
of particular interest to them, and to discuss

recommendations with members of the appropriate adult committee.

c) Secure endorsement. The proposed plan must be presented to the appropriate body for endorsement. This may involve the governing body of your own congregation, the local council of churches, the city council, or the county board—depending upon the scope of your plan. This body must also furnish or approve plans for securing funds to cover the cost of the survey. Even if no professional help is employed, there will be the expenses of postage, long-distance telephone calls, mimeographing materials, and gratuities to consultants.

d) Determine available assistance. In suggesting some advantages of a community self-appraisal, reference was made to local, state, and national departments and agencies that are in position to furnish valuable assistance. Just what help is available from these sources should be determined. Whether this exploration should be made before the proposal is presented to the governing bodies for endorsement may be a matter of strategy. The church, city, or county "fathers" may be more willing to endorse the plan if they know what outside help is available. On the other hand, it may be easier to secure the promise of such help if the plan already has official endorsement.

The work of the planning committee is complete when the plan has been endorsed, committees have been appointed, and such information as has been accumulated is turned over to the steering committee. Of course, many of the members of the planning committee will probably continue to serve in some other capacity.

The statement of need and purpose referred to above may be evolved from the following statement. The portions enclosed in quotation marks are quoted from the foreword of the report of the Waukesha County self-appraisal survey:

"All children and youth face problems in the process of growing up to adulthood. Most of them, with the help of loving and understanding parents, and through their usual contacts with church, school, and leisure time agencies, overcome these problems and become mature and well-adjusted men and women." [4]

Some, however, have exceptional problems that are not readily solved through their usual contacts. Some have impairment of vision, hearing, or speech. Some are mentally retarded. Some have special problems resulting from cerebral palsy, polio, epilepsy, muscular dystrophy, and other such limiting conditions. Still others have problems because they have unusual abilities that are not challenged or developed. In addition, disease and accidents create unusual problems for adults. Furthermore, among both adults and children there are many who are handicapped by emotional problems or social maladjustment.

"It is important for the community, through its many agencies and organizations, not only to make available, but to make certain that the child, youth, or his parents receive the help needed."

It is proposed that this church (or community) conduct a self-appraisal study. Its purposes should be to discover the needs of children, youth, and those of all ages who are handicapped; to determine what services, programs, and facilities are available for meeting these needs, "wherein they can be improved, or, if they are entirely lacking, how they can be established." Because early contact is all-important, since "problems can be handled more easily before undesirable behavior patterns become firmly established," the emphasis should be upon services for children and youth, but the needs of the adult and particularly the aged should not be overlooked. Because of the variety of problems that may be encountered, it is believed that "the schools, churches, health, welfare, and leisure-time agencies, libraries, law-enforcement agencies, and the juvenile court

---

[4] *Ibid.*, foreword.

and its services, all play an important part in trying to meet the needs of children and youth" and all should be involved in the study.

Making the Survey

Your local steering committee should determine the best way to collect the needed data. Detailed suggestions concerning data to be gathered and areas to be explored are given in a forty-eight-page booklet, *How to Conduct a Self-Survey of Special Education Needs.*[5] Letters and forms that may be adapted to local needs or reproduced for your use are also included. This booklet is an excellent guide for both the committee on schools and for the committee on church and family life.

Preliminary steps. Some information should be assembled and studied before your intensive survey is launched. If a

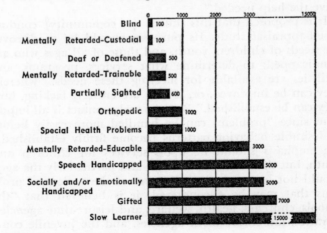

Estimated Number of Exceptional Persons in the United States Among Each 100,000

Blind	100
Mentally Retarded-Custodial	100
Deaf or Deafened	500
Mentally Retarded-Trainable	500
Partially Sighted	600
Orthopedic	1000
Special Health Problems	1000
Mentally Retarded-Educable	3000
Speech Handicapped	5000
Socially and/or Emotionally Handicapped	5000
Gifted	7000
Slow Learner	15000

---

[5] Out of print, but available in some libraries.

committee gathers information concerning the needs of special education in the public schools, as well as the services that are available, the committee on church and family life will be able to utilize it. If the committee does not, the church committee will need to assemble the following information.

1. *General population.*
   a) Total population of the area.
   b) Number of children enrolled in public schools (elementary, junior high school, senior high school).
   c) Number of children enrolled in private or parochial schools (elementary, junior high school, senior high school).
   d) Number of preschool children. (The school census may provide this information.)
   e) How many of these children attend Sunday schools? (This figure should be broken down by congregations and by age groups.)
2. *Persons with exceptional needs.*
   On the basis of the population, how many persons would you expect to find with each type of exceptionality in each age group?

CLASSIFICATION	INCIDENCE
Mentally Retarded-Custodial	0.1%
Mentally Retarded-Trainable	0.5%
Mentally Retarded-Educable	3.0%
Slow Learner	15.0%
Gifted	7.0%
Speech Handicapped	5.0%
Hard of Hearing	3.0%
Deaf or Deafened	0.5%
Partially Sighted	0.6%
Blind	0.1%
Orthopedic	1.0%
Special Health Problems	1.0%
Socially and/or Emotionally Handicapped	5.0%

As was explained in the preceding chapter, the percentages given are estimates only. They do not furnish an accurate prediction of the number of exceptional persons who will be found in your community. Many persons who are exceptional have more than one handicap, which accounts for the staggering figure indicated by the sum of the percentages listed above. Actually, 15 per cent of the population is probably a closer estimate of the total number of exceptional persons to be found in a community. It should also be noted that most of these figures apply to school-age children. The percentages for blindness and deafness increase rapidly as older age groups are included. Your community may have fewer of one exceptionality than the prediction would indicate; on the other hand, you may have more of others. However, this estimate will give you some idea of the probable scope of the problem.

Another check on your estimate may be made by finding out how many exceptional children have been identified by the public schools. School officials should not be asked to give you the names of children who have been identified as exceptional. This involves professional ethics. The school officials may, however, tell you the number of children identified, the age groups, and the school district in which they reside. It will be even more helpful if you can determine the means of identification, for you may place more confidence in the results of professional evaluation than you can in a teacher's impressions. (Remember, many children who are thought to be retarded are actually hard of hearing, emotionally disturbed, brain damaged, or visually impaired.)

You should also find out how many exceptional persons have been identified by the public health nurse and/or the welfare department.

Have your church-school teachers identify as many persons as they can who have exceptional needs, both in and outside the church school.

This information should provide you with an estimate

of the number of persons you will be trying to locate in your survey.

Conducting Your Survey. You may want to conduct your search for exceptional persons as a part of a religious survey. Whether you are conducting the survey as an activity of your own congregation or as an interdenominational project, all of the people who are to participate should meet for a period of instruction and planning. Some of the areas you will need to cover in this meeting are discussed in the following paragraphs.

1. The "surveyors" should be divided into teams. A definite assignment of the area to be covered should be made to each team, so there will be no overlapping or omissions.

2. If this is part of a community self-appraisal effort, the whole program should be briefly discussed. Emphasis should be placed upon the responsibility of the church to serve the religious needs of *all* people—particularly the people with exceptional needs. Although it is improbable that all of the discovered needs will be provided for at once, it is necessary to determine all needs in order to plan wisely. It is hoped that all needs will eventually be met.

3. The card or report form to be used should be presented and discussed.

4. Since the success of this survey will depend in large measure upon the tact and skill of the interviewer, it would be helpful to have a social worker (who has both professional preparation and experience in interviewing) talk to the group about some of the principles involved. It would also be helpful to have selected teams conduct "interviews" before the group. After the "interview" the good points should be stressed by a competent evaluator or by members of the group, and ways for improving the interview should be suggested.

5. Anticipate some of the difficulties that may be encountered, and discuss possible ways of handling them. For example, interviewers are almost certain to hear such comments as: "This is the first time anyone from the church has

called except to ask for money." Or, "The minister never calls on us." Or, "When I was in the hospital this minister and that minister came to see me, but our pastor never came near." They may also encounter the question, "How much is this going to cost?" Interviewers may handle these and other questions and criticisms more effectively if they have talked them over ahead of time.

If no social worker is available to help as suggested above, the following suggestions to interviewers may be helpful:

1. State the purpose of your visit. You might say something like this, "As you probably know, Center City is making a study of services for children and youth, including those with exceptional needs. We know that all children face problems in growing up. Some children and some adults have exceptional problems. It is important for the entire community to discover how well these needs are being met and to try to supply whatever services are needed. Various committees are at work studying many different aspects of the problem. We are working with the committee on the church and family life. We want to extend the services of the church to everyone. We need to find out just how well churches are fulfilling their obligations and what can be done to improve the services. If there are people, either children or adults, who do not attend church because they cannot hear, or cannot see, or are unable to get to church, we want to find them and try to find a way of serving them."

2. As you proceed with the interview, give the person being interviewed a chance to talk. If the church or its program is criticized, listen! Reasonable or unreasonable, you will not be able to help the situation unless you know just how the person feels and what he professes to believe. Don't be on the defensive! Don't interrupt to defend or to contradict, or even to agree! Just listen. This will not be easy. It *is* important.

3. In discussing the children you will have an opportunity to get indications as to whether a child is handi-

100

capped. He may be eight years old and not in school. He may be ten years old and in the second grade. He may go to a special school or a special room.

You will want to check the results of your survey against the data gathered from the schools and public health agencies. No matter how carefully and thoroughly you plan the survey, the chances are you will miss some persons who have exceptional needs. You will want to be continually alert in your efforts to find and include them in the church's program.

Using the data. The next step is to analyze your findings. First, sort the survey cards or report forms according to denominational preference or membership. Next, separate each denominational group into separate groups for each kind of exceptionality. Then divide those with each exceptionality into age groups. These "age groups" may correspond with your church-school groupings (primary, junior, junior high, senior high, older youth, adults) or with the public-school groupings (preschool, elementary, junior high school, senior high school). For your next step, take a large sheet of paper and rule off two more columns than the number of congregations participating in the survey. Beginning at the left, head the first column "Exceptionality," the second "Total Number," the remaining columns are headed by the names of the congregations participating. These may be grouped by denominations (Baptist: First Baptist, Tenth St. Baptist, and so forth), or by areas in the community (North Side, Central, West Side, and so forth).

In the left column, under "Exceptionality," enter the designation for each type of exceptionality. Under each exceptionality, list the age groupings that you decided to use (primary, junior, junior high, and so forth). Then, in appropriate columns, enter the proper number. A map will be helpful in locating the exceptional persons you have identified, particularly if you are covering a large area. Use a different color map tack for each exceptionality. If you wish, all of your cards may be numbered and the tack may

101

be stuck through a small disk of paper on which a corresponding number is written. This will enable you to quickly identify the individual represented on your map by a particular tack. The preparation of such a map will enable you to see at a glance the distribution of the persons needing special services. It will also serve as a good visual aid when you discuss proposed plans with various groups.

Now we are ready to give consideration to the preparation of a master plan of services. Perhaps you will need two special classes for children who are mentally-retarded-trainable (severely retarded). You may want to recommend that children who are mentally-retarded-educable should be integrated with regular classes. There may be enough children who are not attending church school because they need special transportation to justify consideration of using a bus. There may be enough children who are deaf to warrant establishing a special class. Whatever the needs, you will want to draw up a master plan, even though it may be years before all of the plan can be implemented and all needs met.

The next step is to propose an answer to the question, "What shall we do now?" The number of persons in each group, the availability of space, the availability of a qualified teacher, the need for special equipment, and the availability of funds are all factors that must be considered in deciding on your first move. No one can answer these questions for you. They must be worked out in the light of your desire to serve, the needs of the individuals, and the limitations of your resources. Your master plan need not be concerned with any limitations. Since we believe that it surely is God's will that additional services should be provided, we will find ways to secure the space, the money, and the leadership. Nor should we be satisfied until all needs are being met. But what we can do now may be limited by practical considerations. You will want to consider them thoughtfully and prayerfully, and then move confidently ahead.

102

CHAPTER V

Getting Ready

IF YOUR PLANS ARE TO BE REALIZED IN YOUR CHURCH, THE entire congregation must not only accept, but sympathetically and actively endorse the plans. Do you need money for a wheelchair ramp or a group hearing aid? Do you need to build additional classrooms? It will be virtually impossible to obtain the necessary appropriation unless members of the congregation are aware of the needs and accept the responsibility of providing for them.

Meeting exceptional needs is more than a responsibility; it is a challenge to serve God's children. Before you say, "But we can't afford it!" let us pause for a moment. In a small community there is a church that has a beautiful sanctuary and a fine education building—all air conditioned. The chairman of the finance committee told me that if members of that congregation gave only half of a tithe to the church the annual budget would be fully met in less than six months! Would this be true in your church? Are the members of your congregation tithing? Are they giving sacrificially? Perhaps, as a part of our long-range planning, we should include some emphasis on stewardship.

Actually, financing provisions for exceptional needs has a very simple answer. Let us turn our attention to a more complex problem.

Reactions That Compound the Problems

Culturally and legally we recognize the dignity and worth of each individual and his right to the kind of education that will help him become a well-adjusted, contributing

103

member of society. Yet individually we often react in ways that compound the problems of the person with a handicap. Let us look at some of the evidence:

The creators of movie cartoons and so-called "comic strips" apparently believe that the general public finds stuttering amusing. Other reactions of "the public" to persons with speech problems were reported in Chapter III.

We see the "silly grin" and the drooling of the person who has cerebral palsy, but many of us do not know that the person finds it impossible to make the co-ordinated muscular movements of swallowing, and the twisted grin is only further evidence of the lack of muscular control.

Jim was expelled from school as a troublemaker. Tests revealed that the boy was mentally handicapped. Transferred to a room with others of similar ability, he soon became a co-operative, hard-working boy who won the grand prize in a school-wide miniature garden contest.

Jake was thought to be lazy, a delinquent. Investigation revealed that he had high intelligence and was bored by regular class lessons. The assignment of work at the level of his ability and companionship with boys of similar ability helped solve his problem.

Efforts were made to enroll Marie in a class for the mentally retarded. Tests revealed that she had normal intelligence but was handicapped by an emotional problem. She was referred to a child guidance clinic.

Jill was listless and inattentive in the classroom, boisterous and overly aggressive on the playground—quite typical behavior for a child with a hearing loss.

Jerry adjusted his heavy braces so that he could sit down, and then said, "I don't blame them for not playing with me, but I'll never forgive them for pushing me down in the mud and then laughing because I couldn't get up."

"I couldn't come to school," said Frank, "until I promised the doctor I wouldn't run or go up steps. I tried to tell the fellows, but they call me 'sissy.' They won't even play checkers with me. I could beat some of them at checkers."

"I dread going downtown," said Alice. "People either turn their heads and try to pretend they aren't staring at me, or they give me a pitying look and a sick smile. I don't know which is worse." (Alice has cerebral palsy.)

"You'd think cleft palate was contagious, the way people act," Mildred muttered. "People sure are stupid—and hateful."

"I've learned not to try to make friends with children. Their mothers always rush in as though they were rescuing their children from an ogre. It's not my fault the surgeons did such a poor job on my lip and nose."

Anyone who has worked with persons who are exceptional could duplicate these comments—and add many more. A lack of understanding is probably the chief reason for these handicapping reactions to handicapping conditions. Lack of familiarity with the handicap and lack of information often result in rejection and other primitive reactions.

Often we can prepare a class for the enrollment of an exceptional person by talking it over in advance. A frank discussion of individual differences and of the help that may be needed in this particular instance is all that is required, in many cases, to enlist the help of the pupils in making the person with a difference feel welcome.

Sometimes, however, parents object to having their "normal" child in a class with a child who is in some way deformed, subject to epileptic seizures, or is otherwise "different." Such an attitude probably reflects the parents' lack of understanding. But, remembering our own reactions to certain differences, we can appreciate how the parents feel without approving of the attitude. Some consultants believe that a survey (discussed in the preceding chapter) should include questions concerning the attitudes of church members toward various exceptionalities. At any rate, the attitudes of parents constitute a problem that cannot be escaped.

These attitudes *can* be changed, and *must* be changed.

Unless the person who is exceptional is made to feel welcome and accepted, there is little to be gained by providing special classrooms and equipment.

Creating Attitude of Acceptance

Our first step in getting ready to launch a plan for special services is to educate the congregation and create an attitude of acceptance. Here are some suggestions. They are numbered so that you may more readily refer to them in your discussion.

1. The minister may use as illustrations in his sermons stories of persons who are handicapped and their achievements.

2. The minister may preach a sermon, or series of sermons in which he emphasizes different exceptionalities: (a) Christian attitudes toward differences; (b) such texts as "Love thy neighbor"; "I was a stranger"; or "A cup of cold water"; (c) the church's responsibility toward persons with handicaps.

3. Arrange for a program to be presented in the church or church school by a class or school for persons who are handicapped. I have seen good dramatic and musical programs presented by the visually handicapped and an entertaining program of music and novelty numbers by children who are mentally retarded.

4. Have national, state, or local representatives of organizations devoted to work with handicapped or exceptional persons talk to various church groups.

5. Use films dealing with different exceptionalities. Your state board of health, state department of education (or special education), or your state university department of audio-visual aids or department of special education will be able to suggest appropriate films. Many of the organizations listed under "Sources of Assistance" in the Appendix have lists of recommended films available. Most states and state universities also have film libraries. In some instances

films may be obtained with no charge except postage; in other instances, a small fee is charged.

6. Locate handicapped persons in your community who are good speakers or have interesting jobs and have them appear on programs in the church.

7. Help parents of exceptional children to get acquainted and to organize (perhaps a chapter of the Association for Retarded Children or United Cerebral Palsy). You'll discover that many of these parents are well informed concerning some exceptionalities and others are eager to learn. Parents will have some valuable suggestions for creating better understanding.

8. Organize a study group or reading circle to learn more

Encourage the parents of exceptional children to form an organization—to discuss mutual problems, gain insights, and develop more objective attitudes.

about special education. Members may report on books or chapters of books, or speakers may be invited.

9. Invite the teacher of a special class in the public schools or the principal to give a talk.

10. Invite the pastor, church-school superintendent, or teacher from a church in a neighboring community where a church is serving exceptional persons to speak to your church groups.

11. Invite the judge of juvenile court or a social worker to talk about the importance of recognizing individual differences.

12. Present the results of your survey to various church groups.

13. Inform yourself more fully concerning one or more types of exceptionality, so that you will be able to enter into a discussion intelligently. You'll find innumerable opportunities to bring the topic into conversations, thus contributing to the knowledge of your friends and giving them the facts that may help them to modify their attitudes. You may want to read *How to Conquer Your Handicap,* by Marie Beynon Ray [1] and *Give Us the Tools,* by Henry Viscardi, Jr. [2] These, and other books, will help you appreciate the way in which handicaps have been overcome and will convince you that many severe limitations need not constitute insurmountable handicaps. As you become familiar with the life stories, the problems, and the victories of exceptional persons, you will find that you are looking beyond the handicap to the person.

When the public—in particular your congregation—is able to look beyond the speech defect, the crippled limb, the emotional problem, and see the person; when they are able to accept what they see as a child of God, a human being of dignity and worth; then you will be ready to move ahead with your plans. Furthermore, you can be confident

---

[1] (New York: Bobbs-Merrill Co., 1948.)

[2] Eriksan-Taplinger Co., Inc., 119 W. 57th Street, New York 19, N. Y., and condensed in the *Reader's Digest,* November, 1959.

of gaining the co-operation of the congregation and of providing an atmosphere of understanding and acceptance.

If You Use Lecturers

If you plan to have a lecture or series of lectures, the following suggestions may be helpful.

1. Before you invite a guest speaker, try to determine whether he is a good speaker. A man may be an excellent administrator or the author of an excellent book, and still not be a good speaker. If such is the case, you may want to limit him to a ten- or fifteen-minute talk and ask him to serve as a consultant or a participant in a group or panel discussion.

2. If you invite a guest lecturer who has a reputation as a good speaker, be sure to give him adequate time. It may look impressive to have several "name" speakers on an evening's program, but you don't have time to receive what each has to offer. Be extremely cautious in scheduling more than one speaker for an evening.

3. Be sure that the speakers are informed of any time limits and that the chairman has been instructed to adhere strictly to the time schedule.

4. Guard against "overloading" the program with hymns, special music, unrelated announcements, or long introductions.

5. It is often desirable to allow time for questioning the speaker. Some experts are much more effective when answering questions that deal with specific problems than when giving formal addresses. Often audiences like to ask for clarification of points made in the address or for information pertinent to the local situation.

6. If you have a question-and-answer period, the procedures or "rules" should be explicitly stated. For example: "The person recognized by the chairman will please stand and identify himself. Speakers from the floor will be limited to one minute." Another method of conducting the ques-

tion period is to ask members of the audience to write their questions. After the address, the questions are collected. The chairman (or others) may sort the questions and organize them. This enables the chairman to say, "This question has been asked by several people." Or, "Here are two questions that are closely related."

7. If you make use of some of the excellent films dealing with exceptionalities you will want to (a) have someone introduce the film; (b) have someone comment on the film after it has been shown; (c) have someone ready to serve as chairman for a discussion of the film; and (d) have someone serve as a consultant to answer questions that arise during the discussion. Those who work a great deal with audio-visuals agree that much of the effectiveness of a film is lost unless some of the above procedures are followed.

8. Only if a speaker requests that a film be shown on the evening that he speaks should it be scheduled. If you want to show a film which deals with the subject the speaker is to present, it may be wise to ask him whether he would suggest that the film be shown on a night preceding or following his address.

9. You may want to plan a series of meetings. Whether they should be weekly or monthly, and whether they should be community-wide or sponsored by various congregations must be decided in the light of local conditions. You may decide on a combination. For example: begin with a series of congregational meetings to develop interest, then have a series of community-wide meetings announcing "name speakers," and follow this with more congregational meetings to work out your own church's program.

10. Be sure that meetings are well publicized. Don't overlook the effectiveness of personal word-of-mouth invitations.

11. Choose the place of meeting wisely. Most of us are depressed if we go to a meeting and find "only a handful" there. Remember, a "handful" looks much larger in a

small room than in a large auditorium. It may be wise to schedule the meetings for a relatively small room, but have a larger room available nearby. It is good publicity to announce that it was necessary to move to larger quarters.

12. If you have community-wide meetings you will have more sources of funds available (and you will need some money to defray the costs of speakers, films, and publicity even if the auditorium is free). Not only will you be able to call upon each of the co-operating congregations for support, but the P.T.A., the service clubs, and other organizations discovered in your survey to be interested in exceptional persons should all be given an opportunity to help. Other advantages of the community-wide meetings will be discussed in Chapter IX, which deals with the development of programs outside the church.

Whether or not you use any of the suggestions offered in this chapter is unimportant. It is important that you (1) increase your congregation's understanding of exceptionalities; (2) create an attitude of acceptance and appreciation of persons who are handicapped; and (3) develop an awareness of needs and a Christian sense of responsibility for providing needed services. These are the important aspects of "getting ready."

No improvement in diagnostic techniques, no discovery of new therapeutic methods will do as much to relieve the heartache of the person with a handicap as will the understanding acceptance that you can provide.

111

CHAPTER VI

Serving Them in the Church

IF WE RECOGNIZE ALL PEOPLE AS GOD'S CHILDREN AND OUR brothers in Christ we are actively interested in providing for all of their needs. The primary responsibility for meeting some of the needs rests upon our schools; other needs can be met only by community-sponsored services. As citizens of the community, we are responsible for providing the services needed in the schools and in the community. We will consider our responsibilities outside the church in Chapter IX. In this chapter we will discuss plans for an adequate program in the church.

In Chapter IV we considered the collection of data that will be needed for planning adequate services for exceptional persons in your community. Let us assume that you have determined the number of persons of various exceptionalities in each age group, and that you have prepared a map so that you can easily locate each of these persons. The map may show, for example, that there are six preschool children who are visually handicapped. Three are Baptists; two are Methodists; and one is a Presbyterian. They all live within a one-mile radius of the Presbyterian church. This kind of information for each type of exceptionality and each age group has been tabulated, and is readily studied on the map. You are now ready to plan.

Sources of Assistance

Many questions will arise on which you will need the best advice available. If the community self-appraisal was made, you have already become acquainted with some of the sources of assistance to which references were made in other chapters. For convenience, a list is presented here.

Local Sources

Supervisor or director of special education in the schools

Teachers of special classes in the public schools

Psychologists, guidance directors, and consultants on the local school staff

Former teachers or administrators of special education programs who now reside in your community

Ministers, Sunday-school teachers, or others who have had some training or experience in special education or in working with handicapped persons

Boy Scout and Girl Scout leaders who have had some experience either in a sustained program or in a summer camp for handicapped children

Personnel from the child guidance clinic, family service agency, public health department, the probation officer, or judge of juvenile court

Local representatives of such organizations as are listed in the Appendix of this book

Directors of Christian education in local churches
Even though these directors may have had no preparation in the area of special education or work with persons who are handicapped, their knowledge of good procedures in Christian education should be helpful. Furthermore, since the recommendations of your committees will affect the total program, the directors of Christian education should be on the planning committee.

Other Than Local Sources

State director or supervisor of special education
Most states have such a position. Sometimes it is under the Department of Education, Department of Health, or Department of Welfare, and sometimes it is a separate department.

Directors of Christian education in other communities where programs for exceptional persons are in operation

113

District, state, or conference directors of Christian education, such as some denominations have

State and national offices of the organizations interested in exceptional persons

These may arrange for a representative to meet with your committee or direct you to a qualified consultant in a nearby community. They will correspond with you, send literature, and may be able to direct you to a not-too-distant church where special programs are in operation.

Personnel from colleges and universities who are well informed in the areas of education for exceptional persons

Denominational publishing houses and the National Council of Churches of Christ

These have been printing an increasing number of articles dealing with various phases of work with persons who are exceptional. They may be able to direct you to pertinent articles or to the authors with whom you may correspond.

Through personal and group conferences or correspondence with the consultants listed, you will be able to secure help in planning your church's work that is based on local needs and local limitations. These consultants should be called on to help outline your master or long-range plans and to help determine the most urgent need that can be met with available resources.

Since local needs and resources will vary greatly, only general principles may be presented here.

Special or Integrated Class?

One question that is sure to arise is: Shall we establish a special class or try to integrate exceptional persons in existing classes?

There are two general principles to guide us. First, we are primarily interested in providing the kind of educational setting that will be best for the person. This means that we want the kind of class that will most adequately meet the exceptional needs of the person under consideration. To determine what this means we must know the person. Remember, within each category of exceptionality there are wide variations. Furthermore, the impaired hearing or the crippled limb must be recognized as a single factor. There are many factors to be weighed, and the relative importance of each will vary from person to person. For each one we must find the answers to such questions as: Where will he be happiest? Where will he have maximum opportunities for developing Christian attitudes and qualities of leadership? Where will he find the joy of "belonging" and the satisfaction of making a contribution to the group? Where will he find the right balance between success and challenge, security and adventure?

One question that is sure to arise is: Shall we establish a special class or try to integrate exceptional persons in existing classes?

These questions can be answered only in terms of one person in a given set of circumstances. First, then, will a special class or an integrated class offer the most to this person?

The second general principle for our guidance is: In general, it is desirable to keep a child in a regular (or integrated) class if he is able to adjust and "hold his own" there. It is good for the child to learn to live with those

115

who do not have his limitations or handicap. Eventually, if he is to be happy, he must learn to distinguish areas where he can compete on an equal basis, areas where he can compete only if allowances are made for his handicap, and areas where he cannot compete. He must learn, too, to set his goals realistically. There will be some areas in which he cannot hope to meet even minimal goals. On the other hand, many people with handicaps accomplish fantastic feats. A totally blind friend of mine remodeled his kitchen, retiled the bathroom, and installed new electrical fixtures (which involved additional wiring in the attic that had to pass inspection). We must not underestimate what some individuals will be able to do, but it is unfair to expect all similarly limited persons to do the same things. We must emphasize individual differences and the necessity of knowing all that can be learned about the person under consideration.

Some persons develop good adjustment based on objective self-evaluation much more readily than do others. We will want to be sure that a child or adult is ready for an integrated class so that the inevitable competition and comparisons will be challenging rather than frustrating or self-devaluating.

In Chapter II we emphasized the need for complete diagnosis that not only attaches a label to a disorder, but states the extent of the limitations and abilities that exist and predicts the development that may be expected. The fact that a child is in a "special class" in a public school is no warranty that a "special class" in the church school is the best answer to his needs. In the first place, although church and public schools have many problems in common, their goals are not the same. Furthermore, "teachers and school officials cannot and should not, with their usual training, try to diagnose exceptional children." [1] So, before accepting

<hr />

[1] John W. Kidd, "Eliminate Guesswork in Assignments to Special Classes," *Educational Administration and Supervision*, Vol. XLV (July, 1959), pp. 220-24. Used by permission of the publishers, Warwick and York, Inc.

the evaluation of the public school, I should like to have a number of questions answered. What are the procedures for assigning a child to a special class? Who makes the decision? On the basis of what information is the decision made?

To determine the best possible educational placement for some persons only a few tests will be needed. For others, many examinations by various diagnosticians will be required. There is no wish to discourage you by building up an unreasonable list of requirements. On the other hand, educational placement is a serious undertaking with far-reaching effects. The right decision may help the person to achieve a desirable change. The wrong decision may result not only in failure to achieve potential development but in further deterioration.

It behooves us, then, to seek and obtain the most competent professional guidance available. If adequate diagnostic services are not available in the community, we should consider ways of obtaining them. (This phase of our responsibility will be considered in Chapter IX.)

Some Examples

Perhaps the consideration of some examples will help us to apply the two principles for determining whether a person should be in a special or regular (integrated) class.

1. Albert is mentally retarded. Socially and emotionally, as well as in learning ability, he is so different from others of his age that he is unable to participate in or benefit from the regular class procedure. He should be in a special class.

2. Bill is mentally retarded. He is not a discipline problem. He gets along well with other children. He enjoys having his parents help him prepare his Sunday school lesson. As a result, he is able to contribute to the discussion. He competes with a fair degree of success in projects and physical activities. He is accepted by the other members of the class, even though they know that he is in a special room

117

in the public school. Bill should remain in the regular class.

3. Carl is mentally retarded. His attention span is short, and he frequently gets into mischief because he is unable to grasp the class discussion. In spite of your efforts to effect a good adjustment, he is the butt of jokes and jibes. He is emotionally and socially immature. He prefers to play with younger children (who are nearer his ability and interest level). Carl should probably be in a special class.

4. Dorothy had poliomyelitis and is confined to a wheel chair. Although a year retarded in her school work, she makes interesting contributions to her Sunday-school class. She is rather well adjusted and generally accepted. Some special provisions (such as a ramp) are needed, but Dorothy should remain in a regular class.

5. Elaine has epilepsy. Occasionally she has a petit mal seizure. She is a little dulled by the medication that controls her seizures, but she keeps up with the class quite satisfactorily. Many of the children have known her for some time and seem quite unconcerned during her seizures (at which times she drops whatever she is holding and exhibits a few twitches of the muscles of the left side). Elaine should probably remain in the regular class.

6. Frank has epilepsy. Although his parents report that he receives his medication regularly, he has several petit mal seizures every Sunday. He likes to come to Sunday school, but he misses the discussion that takes place or the instructions that are given during his attacks. As a result, there must be constant reviewing in order for him to keep up. This irritates the other members of the class and prevents the accomplishment of the lesson goals. The teacher doesn't want to give him up, because he is "such a sweet child" and she "understands him." Frank should probably be in a special class with a small enrollment so that instruction and projects could be on an individual basis.

7. George has a profound hearing loss. He is learning to read lips, but even with a desk-type hearing aid he is not

Often we can prepare a class for the enrollment of an exceptional person by talking it over in advance.

able to follow the lesson. Sometimes he retreats into his private dream world; other times, he tries to entertain himself in ways that interfere with the class. Until he acquires better communication skills he should be in a special class.

8. Helen is blind. She is very immature and cries frequently. She cannot yet read Braille. She is unable to work independently. Helen should probably be in a special class until she develops more self-confidence and social maturity. She may then return to the regular class.

9. Ida has cerebral palsy. Unless stabilized, her arms, legs, and head are in constant motion. She drools a great deal, and her speech is unintelligible although she understands what is said to her. In deciding what is best for her, the ability and attitude of the teacher, as well as the attitude of the other members of the class, must not be overlooked. We can cultivate understanding and acceptance. We cannot force them. In the public school situation a special class is probably the best choice. In the church school we must ask: Which class will offer the child most in terms of religious instruction? personality development? happy adjustment? In most situations the choice may be a special class, while we redouble our efforts to increase understanding and acceptance of individual differences.

119

10. Joe is emotionally and socially maladjusted. He is unable to adjust to or to co-operate with a group. His behavior is such that the class is in constant turmoil. It may be wise to enroll Joe in a special class with three or four other disturbed children. As a working relationship is established and the teacher develops skill in working with these children, others may be added to the group, one at a time. An alternative would be instruction in the home by a visiting teacher until Joe's professional counselor suggests that he return to the class on a trial basis.

In each case, the decision between special and regular (or integrated) class must be based, not on the label attached to the child, but upon his individual characteristics and needs.

As was suggested earlier, (1) we should try to keep a person with exceptional needs in the regular class if, through some modifications, he will be able to adjust to the group and "hold his own" or compete with a fair degree of success, but (2) each person must be individually considered and the decision made on the basis of what is best for him.

The Special Class

In view of these general principles, we may adopt a policy governing special class enrollment. Exceptional persons should be enrolled in special classes only if they meet one or more of these criteria: (1) because of their differences they are unable to adjust to or benefit from the work of the regular class; (2) because of their differences they must have a sheltered environment; (3) they require specialized equipment which cannot be supplied or procedures that are not practical in the regular class.

Since exceptional persons have exceptional needs that will require some modifications of the regular classroom procedure, not more than one or two handicapped persons should be assigned to any one regular class.

Churches that seek to establish special classes to serve persons with exceptional needs will face a variety of problems. There are questions of space, cost of special equipment, and securing qualified teachers. Furthermore, there is the problem of numbers. A church with a Sunday-school enrollment of two hundred may have twenty or thirty persons who are exceptional. If we could group all persons with exceptional needs in one class, even small congregations would be able to solve the problem of numbers. We realize, of course, that grouping all exceptional children in one class may provide a "special class," but this will not provide "special education." Obviously, such heterogeneous grouping of exceptionalities and ages is no solution. It would, of course, make the task of some teachers easier, but it would not meet the needs of these persons who are handicapped.

The members of any class, to receive maximum benefits, should be homogeneous. This does not mean that they must be of the same age, height, visual acuity, or physical ability. It does mean that they must be able to profit from the teaching materials and procedures that may reasonably be used in one class.

The number in any one congregation who meet this criterion may be so small as to make the establishment of a special class impracticable. The choice at first glance seems to be: unhappy adjustment in a regular class or no Christian education. Many communities have asked a different question: Unhappy adjustment in our own church school or interdenominational co-operation? In any interdenominational plan there is the possibility of friction being caused by those who concentrate so on the uniqueness of their -ist or -ism that they lose sight of the great beliefs, background, and goals that we hold in common. But people who are moved by the spirit of Christ to serve "even the least of these" will concentrate on the larger goal; they will ignore some denominational differences, compromise on some, and work around others so that "the sheep may be fed."

121

The division of responsibility for interdenominational special classes, the questions of financial support, and other queries must be solved in the light of local conditions. Some of the decisions will be based on (1) distribution of population and (2) availability of suitable space. Without interchurch co-operation, only the very largest congregations will have enough exceptional persons to form homogeneous groups.

Interchurch Co-operation

There are several possible ways of operating an interdenominational program of classes for exceptional persons. The simplest consists of an informal agreement among the various congregations. For example, the Baptist church might agree to conduct a class for mentally retarded children between eight and twelve years of age; the Presbyterian church, a class for younger children who are mentally retarded; the Methodists, a class for adults whose hearing impairment prevents their integration with a regular class; other churches, classes for other groups.

A more formal program might begin by establishing an interdenominational committee for exceptional persons. Each of the co-operating congregations would be represented. On the committee or board of directors there might well be some of the following types of churchmen: director of special education in the public schools, professor of special education in a nearby college, a pediatrician, a psychologist, a social worker, a public health nurse, a psychiatrist, and others whose professional training and experience enable them to make a contribution to the program.

This group could work out such problems as administration, financing, and housing. It could also serve as a source of guidance and consultation for the teachers of the special classes or teachers of integrated classes. Such a committee could devise a method for equalizing the cost of operating the various classes, for it will cost more to operate some than others. The committee might decide, after computing a budget, to ask each congregation to contribute a set amount, or the amount may be determined by the size of the congregation (which, in the long run, would approximate the ratio of children in the program). Each congregation might include an amount in the annual budget for support of this special program, or, a class or department might take as a project the support of the program. Another alternative would be an interdenominational fund-raising project. If you really want a program, you will find a way of financing it.

Whether persons who are exceptional are in regular classes or special classes, some of them will need special provisions. Some of these provisions have been discussed in Chapter III in connection with the description of the various exceptionalities. The special requirements will, of course, vary with the individual needs of those to be served. Your concerned awareness of problems and abilities will, with the assistance of your consultants, determine the special provisions you need. Here are a few suggestions, just to start your thinking.

Orthopedic Requirements

The National Society for Crippled Children and Adults, in conjunction with the American Standards Association, is preparing a set of standards for the use of those planning for churches, schools, and other buildings where easy access for persons on crutches or in wheel chairs is desirable. If you are contemplating the building of a new church (school, library, or hospital) you will want to send for these suggestions.

Ramps for wheel chairs should be provided whenever possible. Not only is it safer and more convenient to roll a chair up a ramp than to lift it up steps, it is psychologically desirable—the person in the wheel chair feels less dependent

There are numerous ways in which the local church can provide appropriate accommodations for persons with a handicap.

on others and more welcome. A church-school teacher who has muscular dystrophy wrote the following: "I consider stairs a form of discrimination (unintentional though it may be) that absolutely bars a disabled person from church. And barring anyone from a church is certainly not what Christ had in mind. It is not a private club for able-bodied people only. . . . How can I invite my disabled friends to church, and then tell them they will have to get someone to take them up a flight of steps?" Could this be your church?

Special chairs may be needed to make some physically

handicapped persons comfortable. Some persons who have cerebral palsy will need chairs with high backs to help stabilize their heads, or arms to keep them from falling off the chairs. Sometimes a pediatrician or physical therapist will explain how a person's arms or legs should be stabilized with sandbags or straps to help prevent involuntary movement. Plans for special furniture may be secured from a school for the orthopedically handicapped in your area, or from the National Society for Crippled Children and Adults.

Special tables may be needed. Occasionally you may have a person who, because of braces or ankylosis (stiffness of the joints), cannot sit down; he should have a table with a U-shaped cut-out in one side where he can stand. The surface of the table should be at about elbow height to give him some support.

An elevator would be a real convenience in many churches for the aged and the cardiac patient as well as for the orthopedically handicapped. If an elevator cannot be installed in your present building, you may want to keep this in mind when you shart remodeling or planning your new church.

Bilevel parking lots have been utilized in some of the newer churches. With a church built on a hill it is sometimes possible to have parking lots at two levels so that entrance to both upper and lower floors is at ground level with no steps required.

Reserved parking spaces may be provided for those who most need them.

Visually Handicapped Requirements

Adequate light should be provided for all persons, but it is particularly important for those who are visually handicapped. Daylight (but not direct sunlight) should be utilized as much as possible, but there should also be adequate artificial light. Pupils should not face the window, nor should the teacher stand in front of the window while talking to the class. A white ceiling and light-colored, non-glossy walls should be provided. Windows should have two shades mounted about halfway up so that light may be controlled by pulling one shade up and the other down. The shades should overlap in the middle and should be wide enough to keep out light at the edges.

Chalkboards should be blue-green or grey-green (rather than black), and chalk should be of large size and soft. (Good paints for chalkboards are available.)

Tilt-top desks or reading stands are desirable, for visibility is greatly increased when reading material is at the proper angle rather than flat on a table. In addition, these desks encourage good posture.

A Braillewriter for younger blind children and pocket slates for older ones will enable them to make notes, keep track of assignments, important dates, in much the same way that a sighted child uses pencil and paper. These machines will also assist the teacher in the preparation of materials for those who read Braille. Writing in Braille should not frighten you. After all, if blind children can learn it, certainly sighted adults can. The task may be easier if you obtain a copy of *Transcribers' Guide to Standard English Braille,* by B. M. Krebs, published by the New York Guild for the Jewish Blind, or some instruction from a teacher of the blind.

A typewriter with large type (sometimes called bulletin or primer type) will enable the teacher to prepare materials for those who are visually handicapped but are able to read large-type or sightsaving books. Even if only a few of the partially sighted persons can read type of this size, the special typewriter will be worth the investment. (You'll find many other uses for it—preparing materials for the primary department, announcements for the bulletin board, headlines on a mimeographed circular, name tags for meetings, to name a few.)

Paper, pencils, and lettering pens that will be needed by

the children who are visually handicapped are described in Chapter III.

A quiet room is a help to persons who are visually handicapped, for they must depend to a large extent on what they hear. Noise from traffic or other classes may be a serious interference.

Hard of Hearing Requirements

A quiet room, preferably one that is acoustically treated, should be provided for persons with impaired hearing. If the room cannot be acoustically treated, a rug on the floor and draperies on the walls will help to reduce reverberation and external room noises that would interfere with effective use of hearing aids.

Hearing-aid equipment will be needed. Most of the persons who are acoustically handicapped may have their individual wearable-type hearing aids. Even so, there are advantages to having either individual desk-type hearing aids or a group hearing aid in the classroom. These have the advantage of increased volume, higher fidelity, and binaural amplification, so that maximum use may be made of residual hearing. Hearing aids may also be installed in the sanctuary at various locations—not on the front rows!

Good lighting is needed for the person who is hard of hearing (whether or not he wears a hearing aid) so that he may clearly see the teacher's face; otherwise, he cannot read her lips. Shadows on the teacher's face should be avoided. (The person who is hard of hearing cannot read the lips of anyone who stands in front of a window.)

Visual aids of all kinds should be provided. Their skillful use will supplement what is learned "by ear."

Some suggestions concerning curriculum and teaching materials suitable for persons with exceptional needs were discussed in Chapter III. Here are a few additional suggestions.

Other Teaching Materials

Objects that may be handled are better than pictures for the person who is blind or visually handicapped. Any pictures that are used should be in bold, black outline. Pastel colors will present less contrast and are not so easily seen.

If there are special classes in your public-school system, confer with the teachers concerning the vocabulary and interest level of the exceptional children in your class—particularly the children who are mentally retarded. Remember that the child who is mentally handicapped will develop intellectual skills at a slower rate.

Be sure that materials are at the interest level of the children. A ten-year-old boy who is mentally retarded may not be able to read what a first- or second-grade child can read, but his interests will be more mature. To stimulate and hold his attention you may have to prepare your own materials.

Most children who are handicapped need to develop a sense of their own personal worth and a strength of personality that will enable them to meet life situations with emotional balance and stability. Many young people and adults, particularly those who have recently acquired handicaps, have this same need. Materials should be chosen that will help the person toward self-realization, improved relations with others, and an understanding of a Christian's responsibilities.

Avoid "busy work." In some of the special classes work may need to be individualized. Some children may need to color, draw, or paint while the teacher works with others. However, all activities should be directed toward a predetermined goal. This requires planning creatively. If the teacher is concerned with the developmental needs of the child, the special class will be accepted by the parents and respected by the church school as a whole.

Avoid "teaching in a vacuum." This is always desirable;

it is imperative in work with children who are mentally retarded. A concept, to be meaningful, must be applied. Respect for the rights of others, co-operation, sharing—these and other Christian concepts can best be taught through planned group experiences.

Being Christlike involves the good manners that come from kindliness, the emotional poise that comes from an understanding of one's relationship to God and fellow man, and good health that comes from the recognition of the body as God's temple. Particularly in work with children who are mentally retarded, these goals must not be overlooked.

In working with persons who are gifted, the goals mentioned just above are important, but others also need emphasis. Although we must help the gifted child learn to respect others, we must also help him develop his potential abilities. As a supplement, or in lieu of the regular class, gifted children may meet with a teacher who will direct them in reading and study projects. These may be reported to other classes. The gifted children might enter into a research project that could culminate in the writing and production of a biblical play or a play based on the life of a religious leader. Some may use their talents in preparing teaching aids for use in other classes, such as: relief maps, lessons in Braille, and tape-recorded materials for the blind; materials typed on a large-type typewriter or handlettered for the partially sighted, and short dramatizations of Bible stories planned ahead to co-ordinate with lesson units of their own or other classes. A little imagination and creativity will reveal many projects into which the abilities of the gifted children may be channeled.

Group discussions may be utilized to reinforce, from the Christian point of view, the counseling which the exceptional children are presumably receiving in the public school. The school's counseling program will be aimed at helping a child recognize that he has a disability, to face it, and adjust to it. The church school can supplement this counseling with emphasis on ethical and religious principles. To do this effectively, the teacher must be skilled in the techniques of counseling. Group discussions will also reveal situations and problem areas wherein guidance is needed. Lesson units may be built around these areas.

Development of social competency or "effective-living skills" merits attention in your lesson plans. The person who is handicapped needs to understand why he may have difficulty in some situations and what he may do about it. A person who is blind cannot see what others are doing or what is taking place in the chancel of the church. A person who is crippled may be concerned about his inability to kneel or stand at appropriate times during the service. He may be puzzled about how to ask for help when it is needed, or how to refuse it when he does not need it. Acceptable social behavior interpreted, from the Christian viewpoint, in terms of his limitations, along with matters of grooming and etiquette, may be developed through creative dramatics. No eyebrows should be lifted at the inclusion of such subjects in the church-school curriculum. Jesus blessed the loaves and fishes and fed those who had gathered to hear him. Surely, anything we do to help handicapped persons discover richer, happier lives builds future strength for the church.

Basic Needs

Three points have been repeatedly stressed in previous chapters: (1) the importance of making the person who is in some way different feel accepted; (2) the need of each person to succeed, to perform some activities in a praiseworthy fashion, to "win" at something; and (3) the need of each individual—including those who are in some way handicapped—to feel that he is contributing to the group, that he is "pulling his own weight." Closely related to these needs is the suggestion that persons who are handicapped be *enabled and permitted* to contribute to the life and work of the church. In our discussion of various exceptionalities some suggestions were made along these lines. It is not possible to list in these paragraphs all of the ways in which the goals may be reached, nor to review the many helpful articles that have appeared in the various denominational journals; however, this brief list may stimulate your thinking. You may want to appoint a committee to collect as many denominational journals as possible, also the *International Journal of Religious Education,* and assemble all the articles you find that deal with exceptional persons.

Ways They May Find Satisfaction

The following are suggestions as to how persons who are exceptional may achieve satisfaction in contributing to the work of the church. Perhaps you can add to these.

Deaf and Hard of Hearing: mimeograph church bulletins, fold bulletins and address for mailing, fold letters and prepare for mailing, address envelopes, type, take the offering, arrange flowers and decorations, set up tables and chairs, help prepare and serve food, assist in the nursery during church services. (Many adults who are hard of hearing or deaf have children with normal hearing. Certainly they are capable of assisting in the nursery.) On the other side of the coin, we can learn to use the manual or sign language for communicating a friendly greeting or a comment on the weather. Some persons in your church may be willing to become sufficiently proficient in this means of communication to translate the lesson or sermon for the person who is deaf.

Blind and partially sighted: telephone-answering service for the church office, fold letters and prepare for mailing, sing, pray, lead devotions, teach a class, use a list prepared in Braille or large print and telephone committee members, invitations to meetings or parties. Remember my totally blind friend who remodeled his house; and don't underestimate what the person who is blind can do! For our part, we can learn to write in Braille. If a message or lesson material is prepared in Braille or dictated so that a person who is blind may write it in Braille, then a blind person may prepare additional copies in Braille for the use of others who are visually handicapped.

Orthopedically handicapped: read the Scripture lesson or lead devotions, sing, teach a class, lead a discussion, serve as holder of the script for a play, serve as secretary or treasurer, sew costumes, make place cards and decorations, collect and preserve in a scrapbook all pictures and publicity relating to the church, telephone, serve as cashier (selling tickets and making change for church suppers, rummage sales, entertainments), serve at the information desk during conventions, prepare posters, announcements, bulletins.

What can you add to this list? A little imagination coupled with your awareness of the "need to be needed" and the patience to work with the willing but handicapped person as his work gradually improves—these are the ingredients.

This same ingenuity and sensitivity will help you to modify class activities and procedures so that the person who is handicapped can participate. Large crayons may be used by hands that cannot grasp a small pencil. Finger paints may be used instead of crayons. You are going to let the children draw Joseph's coat of many colors? Finger paints may be used to express the feeling of joyous colors, or some pupils may color whole sheets of paper while others cut and paste to form a coat or a whole landscape. If you know your pupils and their abilities you will be able to make many happy adjustments.

Harold Wilke tells an interesting story that bears repeating here.[2] A boy had had rheumatic fever and for the time being was not permitted to take any vigorous exercise. His church-school teacher observed him riding a bicycle so

---

[2] Harold Wilke, "Acceptance of Handicapped Persons," *The Church and the Handicapped*, Virgil E. Foster, ed., pp. 15-18. See bibliography.

slowly that she marveled at how he could keep his balance. At the first opportunity the teacher suggested a bicycle race, but this one was different! The winner would be the boy or girl who rode the slowest without losing his balance. Of course the boy recovering from rheumatic fever won and found great satisfaction in demonstrating that he could do something better than anyone else! No matter how long a list of suggestions is prepared, it could not substitute for the sensitivity and imagination of the teacher in this true story.

The experienced teacher who understands the pupils with whom she works will set long-term as well as immediate goals and will structure the lessons and materials used toward the fulfillment of these goals. She will, however, because she is sensitive to the needs of the pupils, keep the program flexible. Knowing that change and inner growth are usually painfully slow, she will remain poised and optimistic. She will find satisfaction in the knowledge that she is doing her best to meet the needs of some of God's children.

CHAPTER VII

Serving Them Outside the Church

IN THE PRECEDING CHAPTER WE CONSIDERED WAYS IN WHICH the needs of exceptional persons may be met in the church school and the worship service of the church. In this chapter attention will be given to extending our efforts beyond the walls of the church.

Parents Need Help

We have stated several times that many of the problems of the handicapped person result from the attitudes of others, rather than from the handicap itself, and we have stressed the importance of cultivating in the congregation an attitude of acceptance and understanding. It is even more important that parents and families of exceptional children accept the fact that a child is "different," understand the implications of this "difference," and set realistic goals for the child. By assisting parents with these problems we may not only help both parent and child to a happier adjustment, but may draw the whole family into a closer relationship with the church.

Parents are people. They have feelings, aspirations, frustrations, and "blind spots"—like all the rest of us. Becoming the parent of an exceptional child does not automatically provide the knowledge, understanding, attitudes, and skills that will be needed to help the child grow and mature as a person.

Let me briefly mention three parents. An experienced, successful teacher of children who are mentally retarded refuses to have her retarded son enrolled in a special class;

134

she completely ignores all of the evidence. A psychiatrist who specializes in work with children, and is loved by many because of the excellent help she has given them, did not recognize that her own son was maladjusted until he was arrested. The president of an organization that buys hearing aids for children refuses to let his son wear a hearing aid. Yes, parents often have difficulty in recognizing and accepting the fact that a child—*their* child—is "different."

In general, parents are more objective than they were a generation ago and feel freer to discuss problems that arise because of a child's exceptionality. The fact remains, however, that many children who are handicapped are hampered in developing adequate adjustment and maximum use of their potential skills because of rejection, overindulgence, or overprotection by the family. Sometimes the outward evidence of acceptance of the child is but a veneer over deep hostility and resentment. Sometimes, in spite of competent professional diagnosis and prognosis, parents cling to the hope that the child will in time "be all right." Some parents create in the child feelings of anxiety and worthlessness by insisting upon his striving for goals that he cannot attain, or by refusing to let him strive for those he could attain. Parents experience feelings of guilt and disappointment as well as of despair. They need help, not only for the sake of their own mental health, adjustment, and happiness, but because of the tremendous impact their attitudes have on the children in the family.

Parents need information about the handicapping condition, how it will affect their child's learning, development, and emotional reactions, and what vocational opportunities will be available for him. They want to know what services, what help may be obtained. They want to know whether their child will become self-supporting, able to marry and have a family of his own. Will his children have the same handicap? The need is for an adequate program of counseling for both parents and children.

135

What Is Good Counseling?

There are four requirements for good counseling. First, there must be a genuine Christlike love of people and a desire to help. I know a supervisor of special education who would earn an *A* on a written examination, but she finds handicapped children obnoxious. Her own feelings prevent her from effectively helping teachers and parents. No amount of professional preparation can take the place of the Christian attitude of love.

On the other hand, no matter how great our love and our willingness to serve, nothing can take the place of the second requirement—adequate preparation in the field of counseling. How do you go about discovering what attitudes are hidden beneath the socially acceptable behavior? How do you go about changing attitudes? Often more harm than good results from the statement of personal biases or the giving of even the best advice, no matter how reassuring they were intended to be. Resentment and hostility often result from well-meant but inept counseling.

The third requirement is information. The counselor must be well informed in the whole area of exceptionalities —psychology, development, educational procedures, sources of help, etc. Even these three qualifications are not enough.

Fourth, there must be adequate time. Feelings of guilt or hostility do not give way to feelings of acceptance during an hour's conference. Understanding of problems never before encountered (by these parents) is not achieved because an "authority" is quoted. It may require more courage, self-discipline, and practice for Jim to climb stairs than for Bob to catch a forward pass, but it is easy to see that parents will have difficulty in substituting one achievement for the other in their system of values. Helping parents to understand and to feel relaxed with the child who is handicapped, to rejoice with him in each success (trivial as it may be compared to what "normal" children do), and to learn how to help the child solve his problems is too big an assignment for a single interview—often it is too big for a single counselor.

Particularly difficult to counsel with are the parents of children with emotional or social maladjustments, for all too often the parents are involved in the cause of the difficulty. Some parents do not see the problem, and few see themselves as a cause of the problem. Frequently such parents say, "He was all right until he started to school," or "His teacher just doesn't understand him." They reject the help offered by agencies, such as a child guidance clinic or family service, or, if they make the initial contact, withdraw as soon as they learn that they will be involved in the therapy. The church-school teacher should never attempt to play the role of therapist for the parents. She will need to visit with them in order to secure information about the child and to get the parents to co-operate in the program, but she will not try to deal with the emotional problems of the parents.

If, however, the church-school teacher meets the four qualifications for counseling, she will be able to do a great deal toward helping the parents of children who have handicaps. Since all teachers would probably benefit from a course dealing with the problems of counseling, an interdenominational committee might arrange for a nearby college or university to offer an extension course in your community. If this is not practicable, a less formal course may be taught by someone in your community who has had professional preparation in interpersonal relationships. A third possibility is the establishment of scholarships that will enable church-school teachers to secure preparation both in the area of counseling and in special education.

Even with the best preparation available, some otherwise excellent church-school teachers will be incapable of dealing with the problems of counseling. It is important for them to be aware of their limitations and to have information as to whom those in need of such help may be referred.

Helping Parents Adjust

The counseling of even the best-prepared teacher should be supplemented. The adjustment of parents may be furthered in several ways:

1. Several of the community self-appraisal committees will probably recommend the establishment of services such as a child guidance clinic, a family service agency, a school social worker, and school guidance and counseling personnel. The church and family life committee should make similar recommendations, and the churches should give their support to establishing these services. Without them, the attempts of the church to serve exceptional children will be hampered.

2. Church and public school may work together to encourage the parents of exceptional children to form an organization. Membership in such a group would provide opportunity to discuss mutual problems, gain insights, and develop more objective attitudes. There are three advantages in having an organization that includes *all* interested parents. First, many communities will not have enough parents interested in each of the many types of exceptionality to form separate organizations. Second, meeting with parents who have problems different from their own tends to broaden their understanding and deepen their concern. Third, such a group will more readily lend its support to the efforts of the churches, schools, and community to develop a well-balanced, comprehensive program.

The Council for Exceptional Children, an important department of the National Education Association, is composed primarily of those engaged professionally in serving exceptional persons, but (at the time of this writing) 49 per cent of the membership of a local chapter may be composed of parents and other "nonprofessionals." Whether or not your group of parents combines with professional workers to form a local chapter of the C.E.C., they will want to participate in local and regional C.E.C. Conferences and subscribe to the C.E.C. journal, *Exceptional Children*. This journal, published monthly September through May, contains articles on a wide variety of problems, reports on research studies, practical suggestions for teachers, and reviews of pertinent books and articles. The members of the central organization may be divided into interest groups and may be encouraged to affiliate with organizations devoted to their particular area (such as the National Association for Retarded Children, United Cerebral Palsy, and others). These "specialized" organizations have important functions and make significant contributions, but a central or "all-inclusive" organization is needed in order to give impetus to a long-range, comprehensive plan of services.

3. A series of lectures and discussions (as suggested in the preceding chapter) would provide much of the information that parents need in order to understand their child's difference and the effect that it will have on his— and their—life. As the interest becomes stronger, a study series may be devoted to each of the exceptionalities with which your community is concerned.

Whatever the approach used, we must help parents to accept and understand their exceptional child. This is less tangible than building ramps or installing hearing aids, but it is even more important for the exceptional person and the community.

Helping Those in Institutions

In or near many communities are institutions of different kinds: state schools for those who are deaf, blind, or mentally handicapped; rehabilitation centers for those who are mentally ill; penal institutions for juveniles and adults; and homes for the aged or chronically ill. Every congregation of any size has a member of the church family in some kind of institution. Wherever they are, they need to be continuously reminded of our interest and God's love.

Some of our own members may be too far away for us to

visit them or render direct service, but we can keep in touch with them. A copy of the church bulletin or order of worship, a brief note about the activities of the church and its plans, interesting bits of news about people in the church—and don't omit the bits of humor—will help. A letter might be addressed to "Those Away From Home" and be duplicated, with personal notes written at the bottom. Small gifts on birthdays, at Christmas, or on other special occasions would constitute another reminder of our sustained interest.

To facilitate this program a list of names and addresses (along with birth dates) should be maintained. A committee might serve for a year, or various departments or classes might take the responsibility for weekly or monthly letters. However it is handled, we should not miss this opportunity to remind those away from home of our Christian concern and of the comfort, strength, and redemptive love of God.

But what can we do for those who are in institutions within our reach? Listed below are some of the ways that congregations have tried to serve:

1. Provide transportation for those who need it. Many persons in homes for the aged would enjoy attending a church service or social activity. Children in schools for the blind may need transportation to and from the church school and its various functions. Transportation may also be needed to concerts, lectures, or other programs.

2. Worship services, church-school lessons, or other church programs may be recorded on tape and taken to the residents of homes for the aged, to hospitals, or to some others who cannot be transported to the church.

3. Ask the director of the school or institution what you can do toward providing or augmenting religious services. If a chaplain is on the staff, you will probably be referred to him. Songbooks may be needed, a piano, or someone to play the piano; someone may be needed to direct the singing or direct a choir; some special music may be welcomed. Regular worship services may be needed, or perhaps a Bible

study class could be organized. Perhaps some program (religious or secular) would be welcome as an evening's entertainment.

4. If Sunday-school classes are held in a school for the blind, your help may be needed in the preparation of lesson materials in Braille. You can do it. It is slow, to be sure, but it is relatively simple. With a little practice you will become quite adept. (Try sending birthday or Christmas greetings written in Braille to your blind friends. Their appreciation will be out of proportion to your small effort.)

5. Schools for the deaf sometimes conduct their own religious services. You may be able to enrich the services by giving or loaning pictures, filmstrips, or films. (Films should be silent or have added captions, such as foreign films have.) Appropriate reading materials may be welcomed both for religious classes and for the regular library. If the school does not conduct religious services, you may consider employing a person skilled in using the manual language to conduct such services. This would seem to be a venture in which interdenominational co-operation would be possible or, for financial reasons, necessary.

6. In homes for those who are mentally retarded there will be a relatively large group who would profit from religious instruction. The program must be planned in co-operation with the professional personnel of the school. They may suggest that some of the residents would profit most from instruction in very small groups, while others could patricipate in a more formal worship service. Their opinions should be respected.

7. In homes or schools for those who are disturbed or mentally ill there will be some who will benefit from a worship service or a class. The director, or his representative, should be consulted in planning the content and presentation of these services.

8. The services rendered need not be directly related to worship or religious instruction in order to be truly Christian. As was stated earlier, people need to have the gospel

141

of Jesus Christ demonstrated for them and to have its love shown to them. We may need to remind ourselves that few of the references in the Gospels to the teachings of Jesus could be called "formal sermons." On the other hand, you will find it difficult to read very far without finding the record of a loving word or a kindly deed. A concert by the choir, a play, a party with appropriate activities—many things that bring pleasure can demonstrate our Christian concern. Many of the residents of homes for the aged, convalescent homes, hospitals, and tuberculosis sanitariums need someone to read to them, to write letters for them, to play checkers with them, to listen to them. Do these things seem trivial? Try them and see how much they are appreciated. Jesus recognized the importance of doing the little things that are within our power to do. Remember, "Whoever gives to one of these little ones even a cup of cold water . . . he shall not lose his reward." (Matthew 10:42.)

In our discussion of serving persons in institutions we must not forget the staff members. Of course we will want them to feel welcome in our church whenever they can attend, but some must be on duty every Sunday, Christmas, and Thanksgiving. Perhaps they would

The church has an opportunity and an obligation to help those who are returning to the community from a treatment center or other institution. We need to surround such persons with Christian love and concern.

142

appreciate a short service held at the school or institution at a time when they could attend.

Helping Returnees

The church has an opportunity and an obligation to help those who are returning to the community from a treatment center for the mentally ill or other institution. There are always problems of adjustment, and frequently problems of finding employment. If we fulfill our Christian obligations to these people while they are institutionalized, the problem of providing assistance at the time of their return is simplified. They know that we are interested in them; we have demonstrated it. If for some reason we must ask, "When did we see you sick or in prison and did not minister unto you?" we need to examine our attitudes. How do we feel toward the person? A long exposition of the Christian attitude is unnecessary. We know how Jesus would feel and what he would have us do.

First, then, we must examine ourselves. Do we believe in the redemptive love of God? Do we accept this returnee as a brother in Christ? If in some way he has offended us, how many times must we forgive him? Four hundred and ninety! And if we don't? God will not forgive us. How shall we treat him? As we would like to be treated. Whom should we help? The one who is in need. Is one person so important? All-important! (Read the parables of the lost sheep, the lost coin, the lost son; Luke 15:1-32.)

As has been suggested elsewhere, changing our attitudes—or the attitudes of others—is not easy. We are trying to be followers of Jesus, but we live in communities and we tend to reflect the cultural attitudes of the community. It is not easy to change these learned ways of feeling and reacting. From an intellectual viewpoint, I scoff at the idea of a pin bringing good luck; I understand that this way of reacting dates back to a time when pins were scarce and expensive, but emotionally I still react to finding a pin. We know how we ought to react, but we don't react that way. Most of us tend to react unfavorably toward things that we do not understand or are unfamiliar with in terms of our limited experience. Although we recognize that our reactions are "normal" in that many people have the same ones, we further recognize that they are not Christlike, and that disturbs us. It may be desirable for your group to arrange for a series of meetings to be led by a qualified social worker. Under such leadership it will be possible for most earnest workers to talk about their negative attitudes of aversion and rejection. When we discover why we feel as we do, and that other conscientious Christians often feel the same way, it will be easier to develop positive attitudes of acceptance and helpfulness.

Next, we may give some time and attention to improving the attitudes of the community. The dissemination of information about mental illness and its modern treatment may be helpful and necessary. Our own attitudes of acceptance are important. To a large extent the changing of attitudes in the community must be accomplished on a one-to-one basis—in other words, by our own personal contacts.

The third step is a planned program for the psychological support of the returnee. This may involve including him in the worship and recreational programs of the church. It may involve helping him find employment. It may involve co-operation with the social worker of the mental hospital. Some communities have found that a "big brother" program initiated by the church, a service club, or Y.M.C.A. and Y.W.C.A. has been effective in helping the returnee find his place in the church and in the community. As one community uses the "big brother" program, one or more persons are assigned to the returnee without his knowledge. They call on him, invite him to go to church, to a party, to a concert. They go to his home, get him, take him with them. They let him talk. They listen. They convince him that they are interested in him as a person with a future because they genuinely believe that he is a person with a future. As psychologists express it, they give him support. They stand by him until he has again found his place in the community. They help guide him to sources of financial aid if it is needed, to Alcoholics Anonymous if that is appropriate, to sources of counseling—including the minister— and, if it seems best, they help him to a new start in another community.

Our best efforts will not always be successful. But unless we have done our best to do what Jesus would do, we fail in our obligation.

Serving the Homebound Person

Whether a person is confined to his home for a short period or permanently, the church can render a variety of services. The needs will, of course, vary with the person and family involved. Here are a few suggestions:

1. Call often on the person who is homebound (and his family), but don't stay too long. If you are told, "I know he will be glad to see you, but visiting tires him," ask for a definite time limit. It may be three minutes, fifteen minutes, or thirty minutes—but adhere to the suggested time. Explain that you must go but that you will be back.

2. Try to keep the visit pleasant. If the patient wants to talk about his operation or his arthritis, let him. But don't talk about yours.

3. Those who are strong enough may appreciate it if two or more members of the appropriate church-school class call at the same time and discuss the lesson, activities of the class, etc.

4. Tape-record the worship service (or concert) and take it to the homebound person and his family. A little experimenting with an ordinary tape recorder will enable you to make satisfactory recordings. If your church has a public-address system, some member of your church interested in electronics can easily arrange a way for you to "plug in" and record from the microphone used in that system—which

may give you a better recording. Of course the minister will call, but the responsibility for preparing and delivering the recorded service should rest upon a lay committee.

5. Sunday-school lesson materials may be delivered regularly. Sometimes the teacher and one or more class members may visit a person who is homebound and discuss the lesson.

6. A group of young people and adults may offer to read (from the Bible, religious periodicals, or other material) on a regular schedule. Those chosen for this program should be fairly fluent readers. The time must be arranged for the convenience of the household or institution to be visited.

7. Another committee may relieve the parent (or in some cases the child) of the responsibility of staying with the homebound person so that whoever is responsible may attend church services and activities. Such "relief" is also appreciated at a time that will enable the housekeeper to go shopping.

8. Sometimes parents or guardians of persons with exceptional problems are understandably reluctant to leave them with untrained "sitters." You may want to arrange through your public schools or through interdenominational co-operation to train high-school students or others to serve as "sitters" with persons who have exceptional needs. A public health nurse, the local Red Cross, and a pediatrician might co-operate to provide training of this kind. Those who complete the course satisfactorily can be awarded a certificate, and their names should be placed on a register of persons qualified to render this service. Even though a "baby-sitting" fee may be charged, this would be a real service.

9. Transportation may be arranged that will enable some who are otherwise homebound to attend church services. In some cases this will simply mean providing a car. In other cases, a bus or even a truck may be needed. One church transports everyone who can be moved (and wants to attend) to a special presentation of their annual Christ-

mas festival of music. Wheel chairs come in the trunks of cars and willing arms carry chair and occupant up the long flight of steps. Stretchers arrive in station wagons and trucks. So many people have received inspiration from this service that consideration is being given to having a similar Easter service.

10. If transportation is provided (regularly or on special occasions) some thought must be given to those who do the transporting. If a person must be carried, this must be done gently but firmly. If wheel chairs are to be carried up steps, committees must be responsible for having adequate help. Everyone who participates in the program must display an attitude of cheerful, eager helpfulness.

11. Consult a doctor and a public health nurse. They may suggest ways in which you may be of special service.

12. Like all of us, the person who is homebound needs to feel that he is needed. In other words, if we serve all of his needs we must provide some way for him to serve. Sometimes the person may be confined to his home because of such severe or diverse limitations that he is completely helpless. Often, however, the person who is homebound is able to serve the church if we provide the opportunity. Many of the suggestions made concerning persons with various other exceptionalities apply to the person who is confined to his home. Depending upon the nature of the disability, he may be able to address envelopes for various mailing lists and have them ready when they are needed (entire church membership, the official board, various committees). One pastor asks a former schoolteacher to review books for him—sometimes writing brief reviews, sometimes underscoring passages that he should read. Sometimes the work may be so poorly done that it seems to take more time to correct it than to do it yourself, but frequently the quality of the work improves greatly with a little practice and encouragement. Again, awareness of the need to serve, understanding of the abilities that are present, and your own creative imagination will almost

invariably find a way of meeting this important need.

Carrying out these suggestions will not produce explanations about Christianity. They will be demonstrations of Christianity. Is our faith in Christ so great that we really make an effort to bring others to his church, and, failing in that, do we go to the helpless in the name of the Master?

Know Your Resources

Almost as important as having an answer is knowing where to find it. It is important for those who work with exceptional persons to be familiar with all available sources of help and to know how to secure the services that various agencies offer.

Where can you borrow a wheel chair or a pair of crutches? Where can you borrow a hospital bed (to make the care of the patient easier)? How do you secure the help of Alcoholics Anonymous? Who is the president of the local Association for Retarded Children? What is the local Easter Seal Agency able to do? How can vocational training be secured? Who can counsel with distraught parents? We must know the answers to these and similar questions.

The first step toward seeking help for exceptional persons and their families is knowing your resources. The sources of help will vary from community to community. Your community self-appraisal, if you attempt it, will bring to light much of the information you need. In any event, your public health nurse and your school principal will know many of the local sources for everything from psychological evaluation to financial assistance in furnishing hearing aids or glasses. Your welfare department, judge of juvenile court, and vocational rehabilitation center will direct you to other services. Just because someone tells you that a service is not available, don't give up until you have explored every avenue. Many people do not know. In one state many physicians did not know that it was possible to secure a complete neurological examination at no cost to parents who could not pay for it. In one state many school principals did not know that the state would help them conduct a complete hearing conservation program and even furnish an otologist free of charge. Don't think that your list of available services is complete until you have inquired from colleges and universities, and from private, state, and federal agencies. An amazing number of services are available through various channels.

In every state, the District of Columbia, and Puerto Rico

there is a statewide crippled children's service, operated in the framework of the State Department of Health, or Welfare or less frequently as a part of some other state department. This Crippled Children's Service offers to persons under the age of 21 and in need of help, a means of securing diagnosis, hospitalization, surgery, convalescent care, and braces, appliances, and prostheses. Since each state has its own definition of crippling, the types of cases eligible for this assistance vary from one state to another. It is available in all states to eligible orthopedically handicapped children, and those with cleft lip and palate. To varying degrees in the different states, help is given in cases of rheumatic fever, epilepsy, speech disorders, hearing impairment, eye care, and orthodontic problems.

For adults the Division of Vocational Rehabilitation offers broad services in medical care and training for those who are employable, and social security provisions have now been extended to offer a disability pension to those who are unemployable because of serious physical handicap. For the deaf, the blind, the mentally defective, other aid is available, including special training and institutional care.

Supplementing and extending these services in every state and providing many of the facilities from which the tax-supported agencies may purchase care, are the services offered through voluntary agencies, including the societies for crippled children and other private agencies. In some states these societies for crippled

149

children which are affiliated with the National Society for Crippled Children and Adults, Inc. send mobile clinics and traveling therapists into the rural and sparsely populated areas. They operate treatment centers, rehabilitation centers, sheltered workshops, convalescent homes, nursery schools, resident and day camps, parent education programs, and many other services for crippled children and adults. The 2,000 state and local units of the National Society for Crippled Children and Adults offer a rich resource for help, guidance and information.

To find help for a crippled child or adult, then, the church worker should get in touch with the state society for crippled children, the state crippled children's service (usually in the State Department of Health) or the local public health nurse. The State Department of Education will give information and guidance in problems of educational planning, and the state Division of Vocational Rehabilitation is a resource for vocational training and placement.[1]

If you prepare a complete list of available services, including the names and addresses of the agencies, and place the list in the hands of ministers, teachers, and others who will be referring people to these sources, you will make a very real contribution to meeting the needs of exceptional persons.

Make Good Referrals

Knowing where the needed services are to be found is important. It is equally important to know how to refer children and their parents to the agencies that supply the service. Often a referral must be made by designated individuals—perhaps by the public health nurse, the school principal, the family physician, the juvenile judge, or the

[1] Eveline E. Jacobs, "Some Facts About the Handicapped," *The Church and the Handicapped*, Virgil E. Foster, ed., pp. 8-9. Copyright 1954 by the National Council of the Churches of Christ in the U.S.A. Quoted by permission.

parents themselves. You will need to find out what channels to follow in your own state and community.

But knowing how to make a referral involves more than knowing what channels or procedures to follow. For a referral to be successful, parents must follow through and utilize the service offered. The child is primarily the responsibility of the parent. Unfortunately, although there are many laws that protect the parent's rights, there is no law that compels parents to go to a child guidance clinic or even to buy glasses for their child. Whether or not the parent seeks help for the child depends in large measure upon his understanding of and his attitude toward both the problem and the help that is offered. Cousins suggests that there are three steps involved in successful referrals. "They are (1) Teacher self-examination, (2) Parental preparation, and (3) Preparation of the child." [2]

Self-examination is the first step because our reasons for making the referral will not only color our approach to the child and his parents, but will affect our follow-through on the recommendations that may come back to us. Cousins suggests that we ask ourselves:

> Am I considering referral because I am sincerely interested and want to help? Or are my motivations obtained from such factors as over identification with a child (teacher's pet), failure to have really tried to know and understand (possibly due to a dislike of the child or his parents), a wish to punish him or his parents by this referral, a wish to have a particular pupil removed from one's class group (because his problem threatens the teacher), or a desire to know for curiosity's sake alone? [2]

We need to clarify our motivations before proceeding with the referral.

---

[2] Michael J. Cousins, "Skillful Referral of Parents and Children," *Louisiana Schools*, May, 1958, p. 24.

Parental preparation is the second step. It is wise to establish a good relationship with the parent before the question of a referral is raised. Through frequent conferences, the teacher and parents may already have reached the conclusion that their best efforts have been inadequate and that additional help is needed. If this is not the case, it will probably be necessary to hold several conferences focusing on the recognition that a problem exists and that help is needed. The teacher will want to explain what she has done in the child's behalf and encourage the parents to discuss freely their own efforts.

It is wise to let the parent express the need for help. She may ask, "Is there some way to get help?" or, "Do you suppose the child guidance clinic would help?"

> If a parent can thus express a need, it will become her own suggestion or idea and the teacher's role will have been that of helping to meet a real and verbalized need. This is also important legally because the welfare of a child lies *primarily* with his parents; it is important psychologically because it tends to eliminate any feeling a parent may have that something unwanted is being forced upon her.[3]

If the parent cannot be led to verbalize the need, the teacher may raise the question of securing help. It would hardly be wise to bluntly state, "I think your son should have psychological testing," or, "You ought to take Sally to the clinic." But such a comment as, "I understand that there's a service at the college we could inquire about," or, "Some children have been helped by the child guidance clinic; what would you think of asking them?" would permit the parent to make the request. Cousins points out that at this point it is wise for the teacher to listen while the parent talks "draining off tensions which have been building because of the problem itself, your invitation to

---

[3] *Ibid.,* pp. 24-25.

confer, and the actual process of seeking a solution." [4]
Additional conferences, both before and after referral,
should center in the areas of the child's problem,

> the right one has to feel disappointed in one's self or
> offspring, and difficulties that daily exist for all of us.
> No attempt should be made by the teacher to enter
> into the *feelings* of the parent, or his deep acceptance
> of the child's condition. *Never pity!* Parents and child
> sense such feeling immediately. *Do not diagnose.* It
> is well known that with children's problems many
> parents angrily repudiate the first person who
> identifies their child's difficulty. Permit the referral
> source to handle their findings with parents. We must
> not underestimate the emotional forces that are at
> work in the minds of parents. [5]

Preparation of the child is the third step. The parent
should be urged to explain to the child, simply but truth-
fully, that she and the teacher have discussed ways of
getting help so that he will be happier in school or have
more fun with his playmates. Plans should be explained so
that the child knows what to expect. It is reassuring to a
child to know that he is important enough for his parents
and his teacher to make these plans for him. He will be
pleased and further reassured if he knows that at least one
of his parents is going to participate in the program. As
Cousins puts it, "Some academic and behavioral difficulties
have been greatly relieved just by the referral and evaluation procedures." [6]

In the preparation of the child the teacher has two
functions: to answer any questions that the child may have
(being sure that she supports the parent's explanation), and
if there is any likelihood of members of the class learning
about the referral, to explain it to them so that they will
accept it as natural and nonthreatening.

[4] *Ibid.*, p. 25.
[5] *Ibid.*
[6] *Ibid.*

Adequate preparation for and skillful handling of referrals should result in increased use of resources by parents and children.

A good relationship between the church-school teacher and the public- or parochial-school teacher is essential. If one teacher is urging referral through the family physician for a neurological examination and another teacher recommends a psychiatric evaluation, the chances of successful referral are diminished. We must be sure that we are pulling in the same direction.

If the schools have adequate counseling services, the church-school teacher may supplement and reinforce the referral of the school or special education personnel. Even if the church is taking the lead in the field of special education, a valuable ally is to be found in the regular classroom teacher.

In our efforts to meet the needs of exceptional persons, we must utilize every resource.

CHAPTER VIII

The Teacher of the Exceptional Person

JUST YESTERDAY A COLLEAGUE AND I HAD A LENGTHY DISCUSSION concerning an issue you will face: Is it better to start a program immediately with inadequate equipment and unprepared teachers or is it better to wait until you can secure adequate equipment and teachers who are at least minimally prepared? At the end of an hour we laughed and terminated the "argument." We still disagreed. We laughed because we had changed sides during the discussion. Admittedly, there are arguments on both sides of the issue.

Qualities Needed in the Teacher

In many churches the most disturbing problem will probably be finding teachers. What are some of the qualities we will look for in a prospective teacher of persons who are in some way exceptional? The following paragraphs present six characteristics or qualities that are considered essential. Although they are discussed in terms of the teacher of children, they are just as important for the teacher of other age groups.

1. Love of children. Outstanding teachers vary in many respects, but they have this in common: they genuinely love children. We must distinguish between a healthy love of children and a neurotic need for children. Love remains objective and is willing to go to any length for the good of the child; it endures and it disciplines as the needs of the child dictate.

155

I was talking to a teacher of mentally retarded children in Wisconsin about a mother who said, "I know he doesn't behave, but I love him too much to discipline him." The teacher said, "I have a dog; he used to chase cars. But I love him too much to let him get run over. I had to whip him several times, and I hated to. But I loved him so much I had to teach him to stay in the yard."

Of course I'm not suggesting that a good teacher will whip her children! I am suggesting that it is important for us to distinguish between Christlike love of children and various emotional drives that sometimes masquerade as love. No matter what the other qualifications, without love a teacher is no more than "sounding brass, or a tinkling cymbal."

2. Respect for children. Closely allied to the first characteristic is the respect for children as individuals. Children, as individuals, have rights which we must respect. More important, we must respect their personalities and help them to develop their highest potential. Love and respect enable us to see through the handicap to the child. Love and respect enable us to see behavior problems in their proper perspective and to recognize them as symptoms of unmet needs.

3. Creative imagination. The successful teacher of exceptional children must have the creative imagination to improvise, to prepare materials and lessons that will utilize the child's abilities and avenues of learning.

4. Poise. All teachers, but particularly those who work in the church with children who have exceptional problems, should be well adjusted. They should understand their own motives and reactions. Such understanding not only enables them to be more accepting of the behavior and attitudes of others, it provides the basis for poise and graciousness. Because the church-school teacher is mentally healthy, she finds it possible to study objectively the problem confronting her, rather than confuse the issue with her own emotionality.

5. Humility. The church-school teacher should be free

of pride and arrogance. She must be able to learn from the children she teaches and be willing to seek and accept help. She has the responsibility of becoming well informed concerning the needs and characteristics of handicapped children in general and of her own pupils in particular, and of learning the best possible teaching methods. But she will welcome guidance and ideas. Some of the sources of help will be discussed in another section of this chapter.

6. Acceptance. The need for acceptance has been stressed again and again. Because this is of primary importance, acceptance is mentioned here as a qualification for the church-school teacher who will work with those who are handicapped. It is possible to love people, to respect them, to have a creative imagination, to be eager to learn, and even to have tremendous poise and self-control—and still feel uncomfortable in the presence of braces, ill at ease in the presence of a person known to have epilepsy, or repulsed by the physical characteristics associated with some handicapping conditions. When we truly accept a person as he is, understand his problems, appreciate his abilities (as well as his limitations), we feel comfortable with him.

Here are some suggestions, all too briefly stated, that may help increase your acceptance of those who are in some way different: (a) Study the problem. An intellectual understanding of causes and characteristics will not necessarily alter your emotional reactions, but it is the first step in that direction. (b) View motion pictures dealing with the problems of exceptional persons. (c) Observe a group of exceptional persons, such as a class of children who have cerebral palsy, or observe a speech therapist working with a child who has a cleft palate. (d) Observe with the privilege of helping—of doing the things that you feel ready to do, which may at first involve no physical contact. (e) Gradually begin to co-operate with the person in charge of the group. (f) Gradually begin to assume some responsibilities for certain activities of the group or for individuals within the group.

Not everyone is emotionally equipped to work with some types of exceptional needs. Usually, however, the steps suggested above and group discussions led by an experienced social worker will help us to understand, modify, and eliminate our feelings of revulsion and create in their place attitudes of acceptance.

In addition to these general characteristics, what specific competencies are important for those who work with persons who are handicapped? Fortunately, we may profit from the advice of teachers who are experienced in working with children who have exceptional needs. A series of studies was made in which teachers of children who are blind, partially sighted, deaf, or mentally retarded were asked to indicate the relative importance they attached to each item in long lists of competencies. By averaging the importance-ratings made by the teachers, the rank order of each item was determined.

The teacher of exceptional persons will be helped by the counsel of the professionally trained.

Presented here is a list of ten competencies. Each of them is found among the top ten of at least one of the lists referred to above. The only alteration has been the substitution of "exceptional" for "blind," "deaf," or other designation in the original list. Which competencies do you think are of greatest importance for the church-school teacher? What would you add to this list?

Competencies Important for Teachers of Exceptional Persons

1. "The ability to recognize individual differences in each" exceptional person "and to make provisions for them." [1]

2. "The ability to help" exceptional persons "develop socially acceptable patterns of personal hygiene and behavior." [2]

3. "The ability to recognize possible causes of social, educational and emotional maladjustments of individual" exceptional persons, "and to participate in planning a course of action aimed at alleviating them."

4. "The ability to remain objective, while retaining sensitivity and appreciation for limited achievements" made in spite of the handicapping condition.

5. "The ability to help" exceptional persons "develop self-sufficiency in daily living and in planning for the future." [3]

---

[1] R. P. Mackie and L. M. Dunn, *Teachers of Children Who Are Blind,* United States Office of Education Bulletin No. 10, 1955, U. S. Government Printing Office, Washington, D. C., p. 24.

[2] Mackie, *Teachers of Children Who Are Deaf,* United States Office of Education Bulletin No. 6, 1956, U. S. Government Printing Office, Washington, D. C., p. 7.

[3] R. P. Mackie, H. M. Williams, and L. M. Dunn, *Teachers of Children Who Are Mentally Retarded,* U. S. Office of Education, Bulletin No. 3, 1957, U. S. Government Printing Office, Washington, D. C., p. 24.

6. "The ability to create a classroom atmosphere that is free from pressure and conducive to good mental health." [4]

7. "The ability to help" exceptional persons "with respect to their personal attitudes toward their physical handicap."

8. "The ability to encourage and create situations in which" exceptional persons "have an opportunity to associate naturally and freely with 'the normal.' " [5]

9. "The ability to use a wide range of techniques, materials, and methods" in providing a flexible, individual curriculum. [6]

10. "The ability to help parents get information which will assist them in facing the problems arising from having" an exceptional "child in the family." [7]

It is obvious that the four groups of teachers, experienced in work with those who have exceptional needs (or, at least, needs that must be met in exceptional ways) rate as "most important" those competencies that relate to social and emotional development, recognition of individual differences, creation of classroom atmosphere and situations that will contribute to personal adjustment, and recognition of the social and educational implications of the abilities each individual possesses.

Help for Teachers

The lecture series already referred to (Chapter V) as a means of developing better understanding on the part of the public would also serve to help prepare teachers. Ar-

---

[4] R. P. Mackie and E. Cohoe, *Teachers of Children Who Are Partially Seeing*, United States Office of Education Bulletin No. 7, 1956, U. S. Government Printing Office, Washington, D. C., p. 18.

[5] R. P. Mackie and L. M. Dunn, *Teachers of Children Who Are Blind*, *op. cit.*, p. 24.

[6] Mackie, Williams, and Dunn, *Teachers of Children Who Are Mentally Retarded*, *op. cit.*

[7] Mackie, *Teachers of Children Who Are Deaf*, *op. cit.*

rangments might be made for the speaker to have a dinner meeting with the teachers of exceptional children before the public address, and a short session with them after the address. The possibility of scholarships for church-school teachers to enable them to secure specialized training has already been suggested.

If there are no local consultants available (such as teachers of special classes in the public schools, directors of special education programs, teachers of special education courses in local colleges), consultations may be arranged with such persons from neighboring communities or from the appropriate state department.

The national and state conventions of such organizations as the Council for Exceptional Children would constitute short, intensive preparation periods.

The Bibliography of this book contains a list of books and periodicals that will help the teacher prepare for the vital and challenging task of teaching persons with exceptional needs in either an integrated or a special class.

We should not be satisfied until we have competent, adequately prepared teachers for all classes in our church schools. Until that time comes, we must constantly seek ways of improving the skills of our teachers and the quality of instruction. If we provide the opportunities for increasing the knowledge and ability of our teachers, we may begin our work with the exceptional person as soon as we have found teachers who meet the six criteria discussed at the beginning of this chapter: love, respect, creative imagination, poise (mental health), humility (eagerness to learn), and acceptance. With conscientious, prayerful preparation, much may be done toward "unhandicapping the handicapped," so that they may, through a strong Christian faith, find "the peace that passeth understanding."

CHAPTER IX

The Larger View

Whether you conduct a community self-appraisal study or limit your survey to the area served by your own congregation, you will inevitably become aware of problems related to the exceptional person and his needs that cannot be solved by the services of the church. Some larger churches have professional social workers on their staffs, and some provide extensive counseling services. However, most of us belong to congregations that are too small to afford or to utilize the full-time services of a wide range of professionally prepared people.

Several statements have been made in other chapters concerning community services. In this chapter, let us directly attack the problem of securing the diagnostic, remedial, educational, and other programs that are required if the needs of the exceptional person are to be met.

We have repeatedly emphasized the need for thorough diagnosis as a means for determining the abilities, the limitations and the needs of a person, for we cannot wisely direct our efforts toward helping solve problems if we do not have a clear concept of what the problems are. In addition to diagnosis, we need an interpretation of the findings in terms of abilities, limitations, and prognosis so that we may not only plan wisely the best educational procedures but prepare for future social and economic adjustment.

The Church Must Stimulate
Other Agencies

One of the primary responsibilities of the church is the Christian nurture of the individual, but no matter how broadly this term is interpreted, it cannot meet all needs of the exceptional person. There must be such services as those provided by a child guidance clinic, a family service agency, treatment centers for the physically handicapped, special education for the deaf, hard of hearing, blind, visually handicapped, and mentally retarded. There must be speech correctionists to aid those who are handicapped by defective speech.

We cannot shrug our shoulders and say, "We are meeting our responsibilities. Let the schools and other agencies meet theirs." We are responsible for the schools. We determine the programs that the Community Chest or similar organizations will sponsor. A complete program is our responsibility. We will not achieve it overnight. But until needed services are provided in the community we have not met our Christian responsibility. Jesus himself "went about all the cities and villages, teaching in their synagogues, and preaching the gospel of the kingdom, and healing every disease and every infirmity." (Matthew 9:35.) He instructed his followers to "Heal the sick, raise the dead, cleanse lepers, cast out demons" (Matthew 10:8). For "if a brother or sister is ill-clad and in lack of daily food, and one of you says to them, 'Go in peace, be warmed and filled,' without giving them the things needed for the body, what does it profit?" (James 2:15-17.)

The state agencies and departments (welfare, health, education, etc.) will guide you in your efforts to establish needed services, and can tell you what state and federal aids are available. You will, of course, want to enlist the interest and support of the local medical association, welfare agency, public health nurses, school officials, P.T.A. groups, and service clubs. One advantage of expanding your search

163

for exceptional persons who need the church into a community self-appraisal is that the needs for these special services and programs will be recognized and formulated by a study committee composed of a cross section of the community. You will also have the framework for inter-denominational endorsement of efforts to establish additional services.

Beyond the Local Community

In addition to the diagnostic, counseling, remedial, and educational services that must be sponsored by the community, there are other areas in which the church should take the initiative.

Reference has been made to the consultation arranged by the National Council of the Churches of Christ in the U.S.A. Similar conferences, calling upon church leaders and professional workers in the field of exceptional educational services, could be held profitably. Large cities could hold their own conferences. Smaller communities and rural areas could combine on county or district levels. Such meetings would further the exchange of information and provide for discussion of mutual problems, as well as consultation with professionally prepared workers.

As churches begin to work together toward meeting the challenge of serving persons with exceptional needs, there may develop the need for churches to have conference or state consultants on programs for exceptional persons.

As an increasing number of churches strive to meet their Christian responsibilities in this area, there will be increasing need for a publication devoted to the exceptional child in the church school or the church and the exceptional person. In the meantime, some arrangement could be made for the same informative articles to appear in all denominational journals. The various church-school journals carry articles from time to time that are worthy of much wider circulation. One way of increasing your understanding of exceptional problems and discovering how other churches have solved their problems would be to collect all available religious journals and compile into one volume the articles dealing with religious education of exceptional persons.

Another project that could be handled more economically —and probably more adequately—interdenominationally than by each separate congregation is the building of an adequate library of books and periodicals. Although each church may wish to include in its own library some books and pamphlets dealing with each type of exceptionality, there is need for a good reference library that is available to the general public. Most public libraries already have some good materials and will be agreeable to adding to them if you and your committee indicate the need. Your suggestions of books and pamphlets will probably be appreciated by the librarian. Each church-school class and organization might be invited to contribute a volume; service clubs and civic organizations could be asked to contribute books or funds for purchasing them.

The Bibliography (included in the Appendix of this book) will suggest a number of titles with which to begin your collection. To keep abreast of the newest and the most helpful publications in each area, you will want the suggestions of the organizations listed under "Sources of Assistance." Often these organizations will supply (free or at nominal cost) reprints of pertinent articles from a wide variety of professional journals. These reprints include articles aimed at helping parents accept and understand a child with a handicap, articles offering practical suggestions for helping persons who have exceptional needs, and many other articles of interest. For example, just this week I received one little volume containing reprints from nine publications. The cost was only fifty cents! Be sure that you have your church or interdenominational board on the mailing lists of these organizations; you will receive some free materials and many helpful suggestions for developing your reference library.

Through Christian fellowship and participation in the church program of worship and instruction, persons who are handicapped may develop a faith that will sustain them and enrich their lives.

In Conclusion

The person with exceptional problems needs Christ and the church. Through Christian fellowship and participation in the church programs of worship and instruction persons who are handicapped may develop a faith that will sustain them and enrich their lives. In return, the church will benefit from the increased understanding, the skills, and the inspiration that handicapped persons can contribute. Together we will be demonstrating the brotherhood of man and making real one aspect of the kingdom of God.

Whether you make a large beginning or a small one, if you are wisely utilizing available assets you will find joy in the doing. You will find ways of meeting problems as they arise. You will seek additional information from books, journals, and experienced workers. You will make special provisions where they are necessary and possible. Strong arms may have to temporarily replace a ramp. Other adjustments may have to be made. But if, with love and understanding, you welcome the handicapped person into your church and help him become a part of the church's work, you will have done much toward "unhandicapping the handicapped."

166

Appendix

SUBJECT REFERENCE

SOME of the topics are presented as self-contained units, but the material related to some problem areas is found in several different units. The following table will help you locate the various references to the topics listed. (Numbers refer to pages.)

Acceptance, 17, 24, 31-32, 70-72, 157-58.

Counseling, 24-28, 67-69, 79-80, 116, 128, 129-30, 134-39, 144, 150-54.

Changing attitudes, 10-11, 15-17, 23, 105-8, 143-44, 157-58.

Crippled, 23-24, 63-69, 86, 97, 104, 118, 119, 123-25, 130, 132-33, 149-50.

Emotionally disturbed, 72-81, 97, 104, 120.

Homebound, 23, 84-85, 145-48.

Impaired hearing, 42-51, 86, 97, 104, 118-19, 127, 131.

Impaired vision, 23, 52-63, 97, 116, 119, 125-27, 128, 130, 131-32.

Intellectually exceptional, 23, 34-42, 97, 104, 117-18, 128-30.

Speech handicapped, 9, 69-72, 86, 97, 104.

What can they do in the service of the church? 23, 46, 106-7, 129, 131-33, 147.

SOURCES OF ASSISTANCE

IN addition to the sources listed on pp. 113-14, the following organizations provide the assistance indicated by the comments and/or coded symbols that follow each entry.

B—will supply selected bibliographies of books and articles.

C—makes consultative services available.

I—will furnish information concerning available services or local facilities.

J—publishes a journal containing pertinent articles.

L—has local chapters.

P—publishes pamphlets, booklets, etc., on pertinent subjects.

S—provides services (therapy and financial aid is sometimes available either through the national office or through a local chapter if one exists).

General

American Legion National Rehabilitation Program, 1608 K Street, N.W., Washington 6, D. C. Services for veterans and their children.

American National Red Cross, 17th and D Streets, N.W., Washington 6, D. C. S, including instruction in swimming and crafts.

Boy Scouts of America, Inc., New Brunswick, New Jersey. Handbooks on scouting with the handicapped.

Department of Health, Education and Welfare, Office of Vocational Rehabilitation, 330 Independence Avenue, S.W., Washington 25, D. C. Renders a wide variety of services through ninety state and territorial agencies. Write for free list of bulletins.

Girl Scouts of the United States of America, 830 Third Avenue, New York 22, New York. Handbook on scouting with the handicapped.

Goodwill Industries of America, 1229 20th Street, N.W., Washington 6, D. C. Conducts sheltered workshops and job training in 122 cities in the U. S. and in some other countries.

Council for Exceptional Children, 1201 16th Street, N.W., Washington 6, D.C. *An Annotated Directory of Films on the Handicapped,* **J. L.**

Hearing

Alexander Graham Bell Association for the Deaf, 1537 35th Street, N.W., Washington 7, D. C. **P. I.**

American Hearing Society, 919 18th Street, N.W., Washington 6, D. C. Services for the hard of hearing. **J. L. P. B.**

The John Tracy Clinic, 806 West Adams Boulevard, Los Angeles 7, California. Provides a correspondence course for parents of deaf children.

The Volta Bureau for the Deaf, 1537 35th Street, N.W., Washington, D. C. **B. P.** (The largest library on deafness in the United States.)

Vision

American Foundation for the Blind, 15 West 16th Street, New

York 11, New York. Talking and Braille books. Sells aids and appliances for the blind at cost. **C. P. B. I.** A list of books and periodicals in Braille, large print, and recorded.

American Printing House for the Blind, 1839 Frankfort Avenue, Louisville 6, Kentucky. (Talking books, books in large type, appliances.)

Braille Circulating Library, Inc., 2823 West Grace St., Richmond 21, Virginia. Will lend religious books in Braille and "talking books" (long-playing records) free. Catalogue available.

Christian Record Benevolent Association, Inc., 3705 South 48th Street, Lincoln 6, Nebraska.*

Gospel Association for the Blind, Inc., 120 18th Avenue, College Point 56, New York.*

John Milton Society, 160 Fifth Avenue, New York 10, New York.*

National Society for Prevention of Blindness, 1790 Broadway, New York 19, New York. Available free: "Some Suggested Sources of Equipment and Teacher Aids for Partially Seeing Children." Also, inexpensive leaflets for public information.

Crippled

Association for the Aid of Crippled Children, 345 East 46th Street, New York 17, New York. **C. P.**

Muscular Dystrophy Associations of America, Inc., 1790 Broadway, New York 19, New York. **L. S. P. I.**

National Foundation, 301 East 42nd Street, New York 17, New York.

National Multiple Sclerosis Society, 257 Fourth Avenue, New York 10, New York. **I. P. S.**

National Society for Crippled Children and Adults, Inc., 2023 West Ogden Avenue, Chicago 12, Illinois. **B. I. L. P. S.** Of unusual interest are their bulletins suggesting architectural requirements of physically handicapped people.

United Cerebral Palsy Association, Inc., 321 West 44th Street, New York 36, New York. **I. L. P.**

Mental Health

National Association for Mental Health, 10 Columbus Circle, New York 19, New York. **I. J. L. S.**

---

* Publish religious literature and Sunday-school lessons. Send for descriptive literature.

Mental Retardation

American Association on Mental Deficiency, 20 North Street, P.O. Box 96, Willimantic, Connecticut. **I. L. P.**

National Association for Retarded Children, 386 Park Avenue, South, New York 16, New York. **I. L. P. B.**

ACKNOWLEDGMENTS

WE are indebted to several sources for illustrations used in this book. We are glad to acknowledge these sources as follows:

Page 21—From *Your Gifted Child.* Used by permission of Children's Bureau. Social Security Administration.

Page 36—From *The Child Who Is Mentally Retarded.* Used by permission of Children's Bureau. Social Security Administration.

Page 49—From *The Child Who Is Hard of Hearing.* Used by permission of Children's Bureau. Social Security Administration.

Page 56—From *The Child Who Is Mentally Retarded.* Used by permission of Children's Bureau. Social Security Administration.

Page 68—From *The Child With a Missing Arm or Leg.* Used by permission of Children's Bureau. Social Security Administration.

Page 74—From *Your Child's Emotional Health.* Used by permission of Public Affairs Pamphlets.

Page 93—Artist: Clifford Johnston. Used by permission of *The Church School.*

Page 107—Artist: Clifford Johnston. Used by permission of *The Church School.*

Page 119—Artist: Clifford Johnston. Used by permission of *The Church School.*

Page 124—Artist: Clifford Johnston. Used by permission of *The Church School.*

Page 158—From *Your Gifted Child.* Used by permission of Children's Bureau. Social Security Administration.

Bibliography

In addition to the excellent articles appearing in your own and other denominational journals and in the journals of some of the organizations listed above, you will want to have in your library books and pamphlets suitable for both parents and In addition to the excellent articles appearing in your own and teachers. Here are some suggestions. Keep in mind that prices are subject to change at any time.

GENERAL

Audio-Visual Instruction, Vol. 4, No. 2 (February, 1959). National Education Association, 1201 16th Street N. W., Washington 6, D. C. This issue is devoted to work with children who have various handicaps. Classroom Teachers' Department. (25¢.)

Axline, Virginia Mae. *Play Therapy*. Boston: Houghton Mifflin Co., 1947.

Better Living Booklets. Science Research Associates, 259 E. Erie Street, Chicago 11, Illinois. (60¢ each.) Write for list of booklets dealing with problems of children.

Cruickshank, William M., and Johnson, G. Orville (eds.). *Education of Exceptional Children and Youth*. Englewood Cliffs, N. J.: Prentice-Hall, Inc., 1958. Outstanding workers in various areas of exceptionality contributed chapters.

DeHaan, Robert F., and Kough, Jack. *Identifying Children with Special Needs* (Elementary Ed. $2.20) and *Helping Children with Special Needs* (Elementary Ed. $3.25). Science Research Associates, 259 E. Erie Street, Chicago 11, Illinois, 1956. These two volumes prepared for elementary schoolteachers and two similar volumes prepared for secondary schoolteachers contain much that may be applied to the church school.

Foster, Virgil E. (ed.). *The Church and the Handicapped*. Office of Publication and Distribution, National Council of Churches, 475 Riverside Drive, New York 27, New York, 1954. (40¢.) A reprint of nine articles that appeared in the International Journal of Religious Education. Every teacher should read it!

Hymes, James L., Jr. *Understanding Your Child*, New York: Prentice-Hall, Inc., 1952.

Kemp, Charles F. *The Pastor and Community Resources*. St. Louis: The Bethany Press, 1960. $1.50.

Ray, Marie Beynon. *How to Conquer Your Handicaps.* New York: Bobbs-Merrill Co., 1948. Informative and challenging. Out of print.

Teagarden, Florence M. *Child Psychology for Professional Workers.* New York: Prentice-Hall, Inc., 1946. Discusses general characteristics of childhood and of various exceptional groups.

What Is Special About Special Education? Washington: Council for Exceptional Children. A reprint of articles dealing with exceptionalities. National Education Association, Exceptional Children Department, 1953. (80¢.)

INTELLECTUALLY EXCEPTIONAL

Carlson, Bernice Wells, and Ginglend, David R. *Play Activities for the Retarded Child.* New York and Nashville: Abingdon Press, 1961. $4.00.

Kemp, Charles F. *The Church: The Gifted and the Retarded Child.* St. Louis: The Bethany Press, 1958. $3.50.

Lerrigo, Marion O. *The Mentally Retarded and the Church.* Published for the Division of Christian Education, National Council of the Churches of Christ in the U.S.A., by the Office of Publication and Distribution. Available from National Association for Retarded Children, Inc., 1958. (25¢.)

Organizing Religious Classes for Mentally Retarded Children. Board for Parish Education, The Lutheran Church-Missouri Synod, 210 North Broadway, St. Louis 2, Missouri. This 26-page booklet deals with problems of organization, time and place of meeting, planning the church-school session, and offers many practical suggestions.

Petersen, Sigurd D. *Retarded Children: God's Children.* Philadelphia: The Westminster Press, 1960. $3.00.

"Wonder-Full": An In-Service Teacher Training Course for Part-Time Religious Classes for Mentally Retarded Persons. Milwaukee County Association for Retarded Children, 3131 West Liston Avenue, Milwaukee 8, Wisconsin, 1959. ($3.00.)

CEREBRAL PALSY

Cerebral Palsy Equipment. The National Society for Crippled Children and Adults, 2023 West Ogden Street, Chicago 12, Illinois, 1950.

Killilea, Marie L. *Karen.* New York: Prentice-Hall, Inc., 1952. $3.50 The story of a girl who had cerebral palsy.

Stevens, Godfrey D., and Birch, Jack W. *Guidelines for the Future.* United Cerebral Palsy, Inc., New York 37, New York, 321 West 44th Street, 1959. Written for parents and interested laymen. (20¢.)

CRIPPLED

Barker, Roger C., et al. *Adjustment to Physical Handicap and Illness.* Revised edition; New York: Social Science Research Council, 1953.

Bond, L. Donald. *Sunday School and the Handicapped Child.* Reprinted from the December, 1955, issue of *The Crippled Child.* A leaflet available from the National Society for Crippled Children and Adults, 2023 West Ogden Street, Chicago 12, Illinois. 1 to 24 copies, 10¢.

Rose, Anna Perriott. *Room for One More.* Boston: Houghton Mifflin Co., 1950. Written by the mother of six children, one of whom was a crippled boy.

Viscardi, Henry, Jr. *A Man's Stature.* New York: John Day Co., 1952. Autobiography of a man born with malformed legs.

VISION

Abel, Georgie Lee (comp.). *Concerning the Education of Blind Children.* New York: American Foundation for the Blind, 1959. ($1.00.)

———(comp.). *Resources for Teachers of Blind with Sighted Children.* New York: American Foundation for the Blind, 1957. (75¢.)

Chevigny, Hector. *My Eyes Have a Cold Nose.* New Haven, Connecticut: Yale University Press, 1946. Story of one man's adjustment to blindness.

Is Your Child Blind? New York: American Foundation for the Blind, 1951. (15¢.)

Lowenfeld, Barthold. *Our Blind Children.* Springfield, Illinois: Charles C. Thomas, publisher, 1956.

HEARING

Davis, Hallowell (ed.). *Hearing and Deafness,* A Guide for Laymen. New York: Rinehart Books Inc., 1951. Provides an understanding of the problems of the hard of hearing and the deaf person.

Hearing News, official publication of the American Hearing Society, published bimonthly. Subscription: $3.00 per year.

How to Help the Hard of Hearing Child in Your Schoolroom. Prepared by the staff of the New York League for the Hard of Hearing, 480 Lexington Avenue, New York 17, New York, 1955. (25¢.)

If You Have a Deaf Child. Illinois School for Mothers of Deaf Children. University of Illinois, Division of Services for Crippled Children, Springfield, Illinois, 1950. Paper, $1.00.

Keaster, Jacqueline, and Hoversten, Gloria. *Suggestions to the Parents of Children with Hearing Impairments.* American Academy of Ophthalmology and Otolaryngology, 15 Second Street, S. W., Rochester, Minnesota, 1958. Single copy, 50¢. 25 copies, $11.00.

Myklebust, Helmer R. *Your Deaf Child: A Guide for Parents.* Springfield, Illinois: Charles C. Thomas, publisher, 1950.

Ross, Jean. *My Son Has a Hearing Loss.* Reprint No. 310, American Hearing Society, 919 18th Street, N. W., Washington 6, D. C. (10¢.)

EPILEPSY

Child With Epilepsy, The, Folder No. 35. Federal Security Agency, Social Security Administration, Children's Bureau. Washington: Government Printing Office, 1952. (10¢.)

Epileptic Child in Your School, The, Wisconsin Epilepsy League, Inc., 756 North Milwaukee Street, Milwaukee 2, Wisconsin, 1955. 10¢ for single copy. Practical suggestions, including what to do during a seizure, and so forth.

Prognosis: Favorable. The National Epilepsy League, Inc., Room 201-2, 208 North Wells Street, Chicago 6, Illinois. (3½¢.)

EMOTIONALLY DISTURBED

Hymes, James L., Jr. *Behavior and Misbehavior; A Teachers' Guide to Action.* New York: Prentice-Hall, Inc., 1955.

Joseph, Harry, and Zern, Gordon. *The Emotional Problems of Children.* New York: Crown Publishers, 1954. $3.75.

Rogers, Dorothy. *Mental Hygiene in Elementary Education.* Boston: Houghton Mifflin Co., 1957.

SPEECH

Johnson, Wendell. *Speech Problems of Children.* New York: Grune and Stratton, 1950. Written for parents and teachers.

Lassman, Grace Harris. *Language for the Preschool Deaf Child.* New York: Grune and Stratton, 1950. Practical suggestions for parents.

Palmer, Charles E. *Speech and Hearing Problems: A Guide for Teachers and Parents.* Springfield, Illinois: Charles C. Thomas, publisher, 1961.

Schreiber, Flora R. *Your Child's Speech: A Practical Guide for Parents for the First Five Years.* New York: G. P. Putnam's Sons, 1956.

DATE DUE

FEB 5 '75			
FEB 12			
FEB 26 '75			
MAR 11			
APR 9 '75			
MAY 1 '76			
FEB 28 '78			
MAR 6 '80			
3-18-80			
APR 2 '80			
MAY 2 '80			
DEC 15 '80			
OCT 20 '82			
NOV 1 '82			
SEP 21 1984			
MAY 02 1988			
OCT 18 2010			
GAYLORD			PRINTED IN U.S.A.